Attitudes of the Beatitudes

Attitudes of the Beatitudes

R.L Brandt

Bridge Publishing
South Plainfield, NJ

All Scripture references are taken from the King James Version of the Bible unless otherwise noted.

Attitudes of the Beatitudes
ISBN 0-88270-647-0
Library of Congress Catalog Card No. Pending

Published by:
Bridge Publishing Inc.
2500 Hamilton Blvd.
South Plainfield, NJ 07080

Printed in the United States of America.

To my beloved brethren serving on the Executive Presbytery of the Assemblies of God during my tenure there.

These men have contributed immeasurably to my life and ministry, and it has been a high pleasure working with them.

Contents

Foreword

Every word our Lord Jesus spoke should be most precious to those who profess to be His followers. His voice is that of the Chief Shepherd, who often said, *He that hath an ear to hear let him hear*. When He speaks, it is the Master speaking. He is the Builder of the Church, the Bishop and Head of the Church. He bought the Church with His own precious blood. His instructions are for her growth, her protection and for her guidance. Because *no man ever spoke like this Man* we must listen for our profit. One day we shall stand before Him to give account of the stewardship He entrusted to us.

There is no portion of the Holy Scriptures for which mankind expresses so great a reverence as the Sermon on the Mount. While interpreters differ as to its actual message, it is clear that Jesus' design in this sermon was to open to His audience the nature of the Kingdom He had announced He would establish. As Charles Simeon says, "He wanted to rescue the moral law from those false glosses which the Pharisees had put upon it." The general idea was that their Messiah would establish a temporal kingdom under which they would be able to enjoy the highest privileges and blessings. They dreamed of riches and mirth. But the people of the Kingdom Jesus came to introduce, the people He would declare to be blessed, were the poor, the mournful, the meek, the pure in heart and the peacemakers.

My dear friend, R. L. Brandt, has such a sublime and spiritual view of this Kingdom. He writes in his preface, "The Beatitudes are an intricately woven piece of needlework. Each Beatitude, like a single thread, portrays the essential attitude in the believer's progress toward conformity to the image of God's Son. Compositely, the Beatitudes are a skillfully wrought tapestry, depicting the fully adorned followers of the Lord Jesus Christ."

To use a play on words, these are the BE-attitudes, not the DO-attitudes. Jesus Christ is much more concerned about us "being" than He is about us "doing." He said, "You shall BE witnesses," with the emphasis on being.

Robert L. Brandt has dug deeply into the richest treasures of the Sermon on the Mount. He has struck pure gold. From his thorough knowledge of God's Word and his personal experiences in serving God, he has incorporated deep spiritual truths that make for inspiring and joyous reading. After reading *The Attitudes of the Beatitudes,* the reader will have an entirely new comprehension of these words of Jesus.

I have in my library some of the greatest writers of the Church both in the present and in the past, but *The Attitudes of the Beatitudes* ranks among the very top and is perhaps the best of all the author's published works.

—Paul E. Lowenberg

Preface

Understanding the Beatitudes requires the perception that each Beatitude is inseparably related to each of the other Beatitudes and to the Beatitudes as a whole. Even as a tapestry would not be complete without every thread in its proper place, carefully woven into the whole, so not a single Beatitude was intended to stand by itself or apart from all the others.

The Beatitudes are an intricately woven piece of needlework. Each Beatitude, like a single thread, portrays an essential attitude in the believer's progress toward conformity to the image of God's Son. Compositely, the Beatitudes are a skillfully wrought tapestry, depicting the fully adorned follower of the Lord Jesus.

As in the weaving of a tapestry, there must be a starting point — and a finishing point — a final thread — to complete the work of art, so the Beatitudes have their own starting and finishing lines of poignant truth. Each truth is intended to bring the child of God to *the measure of the stature of the fulness of Christ* (Eph. 4:13).

The relationship of the threads in a tapestry is what leads to the end result, culminating in the fulfillment of the artist's dream. When a single thread is omitted or misplaced, the artist's intention is marred or distorted. With the Beatitudes, it is the same. Not a single Beatitude can be omitted or taken out of intended sequence if the Master Artist's objective is to be attained to the ultimate degree in the believer's life. *The Attitudes of the Beatitudes,* when taken together, enable the believer to partake of the fulness of God's blessing.

Introduction

This book is about our attitudes and God's blessings, and how they relate to each other.

In a *Reader's Digest* article, world-famous preacher and author Norman Vincent Peale wrote: "Scientific evidence confirms what intuition tells us: attitude plays an important, sometimes definitive, role in success, or failure. [1]

Addressing the same idea, I once heard a black brother observe, "Your attitudes determine your altitude — the heights you reach in God." I want to hitchhike a ride on that idea and add: "Our attitudes determine the extent to which God's blessings reach us."

The Beatitudes are about God's blessing, and what brings those blessings to us. They are like golden keys to God's treasure house, opening the door to the unfathomable and indescribable blessings of God. Solomon, the wisest man ever, put it this way: *The blessing of the Lord, it maketh rich, and he addeth no sorrow with it* (Prov. 10:22).

The Beatitudes plow up the fertile soil of the human heart and lay the groundwork for God's blessings to come upon us mere mortals.

It is imperative for us to perceive that it is God's passion to bless people. His intention to do this was among His earliest revelations to man. In the first book of the Bible, God spoke to Abram: *Now the Lord had said unto Abram, Get thee out of thy country, and from thy kindred, and from thy father's house, unto a land that I will show thee: And I will make of thee a great nation, and I will bless thee, and make thy name great; and thou shalt be a blessing: and I will bless them that bless thee, and curse him that curseth thee: and in thee shall all families of the earth be blessed* (Gen. 12:1-3).

God's nature is to bless. Satan's is to curse.

The eternal purpose was not so much for man to bless God, as it was for God to bless man. Howbeit, when men are blessed of God, God himself is blessed. Jesus said, *It is more blessed to give than to receive* (Acts 20:35).

Satan's master blow was aimed at alienating man from the level of relationship with God wherein he could experience God's blessings, and Satan did this by seducing earliest man into a state of wrong attitudes.

At the precise moment when the tempter's suggestions were heeded, wrong attitudes were born in man — wrong attitudes toward his Maker, wrong attitudes toward His Word, wrong attitudes in man toward himself. And as early as the first generation, wrong attitudes toward others could be seen in the fractured relationship between Cain and Abel.

"Attitude" is a word that is foreign to the King James Version of the Bible, but the sense of the word is very apparent. Perhaps the term that is closest to a synonym in the King James Version for "attitude" is "spirit."

Attitude, as we will use it, has to do essentially with one's frame of mind, mind-set, the bent of the heart and the posture of the spirit. These are the topics to which Jesus addressed himself in the Beatitudes.

—*R. L. Brandt*

1

On Getting God to Look Your Way

Blessed are the poor in spirit: for theirs is the kingdom of heaven (Matt. 5:3).

What must I do to get God to look my way? How can I get His attention? Isaiah has the answer: *...but to this man will I look, even to him that is poor and of a contrite spirit, and trembleth at my word* (Isa. 66:2).

That is almost parallel to Jesus' first Beatitude: *Blessed are the poor in spirit: for theirs is the kingdom of heaven* (Matt. 5:3).

The blessed man is without question the man toward whom God looks. The word "blessed" has a vibrant and heavenly ring. Jesus' use of the word might better be translated, "Oh, the blessedness of the man!" The word is loaded with meaning — blessed of God; in a state to be desired; filled with life, joy and satisfaction; enviably fortunate; well off; spiritually prosperous.

This, Jesus said, is the portion that belongs to the poor in spirit.

So here we have the starting point, the first thread in the heavenly Artist's tapestry.

Here is the foundation stone for a glorious superstructure. Apart from this basic attitude, it is unlikely that the other necessary attitudes will be attainable to any great degree.

Quite obviously, Jesus was not saying, "Blessed are those with a poor spirit or attitude." Wrong attitudes rob us. They cause us to come short of God's glory and they short-circuit the blessings that He intends for us to have.

The first child born in the human family fell far short of being "poor in spirit." His poor spirit and errant attitude made a murderer of him, and earned for him an inescapable mark (see Gen. 4:15) which he could not cast off until his death. God had said to him, *Why art thou wroth? and why is thy countenance fallen?* (Gen. 4:6). His attitude could not be hidden. And ours cannot be hidden either.

While pastoring my first church I learned a valuable lesson about attitudes. I was ambitious about building a good church and was always searching for ideas to improve what I had. On one occasion I visited a thriving church in another state and there I observed carefully all that was done in the hope of finding new ways for bettering our church. Among other things, I noted that this church used the envelope system of giving, and it occurred to me that this might help develop systematic giving in my congregation and substantially increase our level of income. Admittedly there was a bit of self-interest involved in my thinking. I need to tell you that in the early days of the Pentecostal movement, envelopes were very seldom used.

When I returned home, I set things in motion. Giving envelopes were ordered, promotional materials were gathered and finally I prepared a sermon to introduce this new idea. I did it on a Sunday morning. Mustering all of the selling force my inexperience could produce, I laid the matter before my congregation. But to my chagrin and disappointment, the longer I talked and the harder I pressed, the colder the atmosphere grew, until it was like a January night in Barrow, Alaska.

When the service finally ended I knew all too well that my aspirations had died a sudden and severe death.

"What to do now?" I thought. "What should my attitude be?" I could, of course, exercise my pastoral authority and insist on using the envelope system despite the strong resistance of the people. Thankfully the Lord gave me enough sense to realize that such a course would have been pure folly.

Instead I prayed and pondered. I had so greatly wanted the envelope system, but any hope of it had died. As the week wore on, and I struggled over just what to do, I began sensing the Holy Spirit nudging me. The question pressing upon my spirit was, *Are you as willing not to have the envelope system as you want your people to be willing to have it?* That put things in a whole new light for me. It was not easy to refrain from allowing a wrong attitude to dominate my consideration, but in the end I submitted and told the Lord I was willing to heed His voice.

The following Sunday, as I stood before my people, I told them of my struggle. I acknowledged my defeat from the previous Sunday, and I tried to explain the temptation to develop a poor spirit that I faced. Then I related how the Holy Spirit had dealt with my spirit and how I had come to the place where I was as willing not to have the envelope system as I had wanted them to be willing to have it.

Strangely the atmosphere changed, as if a warm sun had broken through a dark cloud cover. "Now," I said to the people, "we have these envelopes on hand. Will you do me a favor? Will you take them and use them for two or three weeks? After that time, if you want to continue using them, fine. And if not, fine too. The decision is yours."

That same crowd who had frozen up at my original presentation, took the envelopes and began immediately to use them. Amazingly, in two to three weeks, they were testifying about the blessing that had come to them by giving through the envelope system. From then on the envelope system of giving blessed our church.

That experience taught me a most valuable lesson which has remained with me for more than fifty years of ministry. If we can conquer our own temptation toward poor spirits and wrong attitudes, we can also influence others to have right spirits and proper attitudes.

"Poor in spirit" does not necessarily imply economic poverty, but Luke hints at this interpretation when he quotes the Lord as saying: *Blessed be ye poor: for yours is the kingdom of God* (Luke 6:20).

Economic poverty often tends to generate poverty of spirit, whereas wealth often militates against it. Therefore, in the midst of a preacher-promoted doctrine of material prosperity and a society inclined toward materialism, the followers of the Lamb must ever be watchful lest they be victimized by overemphasized truth or false teachings. A genuine biblical perspective will preserve the committed believer from such an error.

Material prosperity for the believer is commonly promoted on the basis of so-called covenant rights and privileges. While it is agreed that the believer does have covenant rights and privileges, it is extremely important for him to understand accurately which covenant applies to him, and what the provisions of that covenant are.

Scriptures project two main covenants — one is the Old Testament; the other is the New Testament. To fail to discern between the two is to fall prey to gross and destructive error. In Hebrews we learn that Jesus *...is the mediator of a better covenant, which was established on better promises* (Heb. 8:6), clearly indicating two covenants — the lesser Old Testament covenant, and the better New Testament covenant.

While the better New Covenant and its provisions are hinted at in the lesser Old Covenant (see Gal. 3:14), they did not appear in their full glory until Jesus came upon the scene.

Paul made it clear that the difference between the two covenants was the difference between the bondwoman Hagar's child and the free woman Sarai's child. It is, he says, the difference between Jerusalem which now is and is in bondage with her children, and the Jerusalem which is above and is free (see Gal. 4:22-31). It is the difference between the natural and the spiritual.

Primarily, the Old Covenant had to do with land and posterity and prosperity and earthly blessings and cursings. Its underpinning was the Law. The New (and better) Covenant has little concern with earthly considerations, except as they may be by-products. But it has everything to do with eternal and invisible values. Grace is its underpinning and its central emphasis is *all spiritual blessings in heavenly places* (Eph. 1:3).

The old is concerned with time, with materialism and with the earthly; the new is concerned with the eternal, the invisible and the heavenly.

Confusion is kindled when people seek to impose upon the New Covenant the provisions of the old, and a tension is generated in the effort to merge the two. Believers become frustrated and disillusioned when attempting to appropriate provisions of a covenant which has been displaced by a better covenant. Thus, to force the idea of material and earthly prosperity upon the New Covenant is to substitute a lesser Old Covenant earthly material prosperity for the better New Covenant spiritual prosperity.

It must be seen that neither material prosperity nor the absence of it can be considered the fruit of the better covenant, for that covenant deals with higher ad better realities than material and earthly things.

Pursuing material prosperity on the basis of covenant relationship is like pursuing the wind. It is like penciling into a contract provisions not included when the contract was negotiated and then trying to enforce them. The end result is folly, frustration and disappointment.

The believer's goal is higher and better. It is spiritual prosperity and the blessings of the Kingdom. Whether or not he is rich or poor is not the issue. He may or may not be endowed with much of this world's goods, depending on life's circumstances. But his eyes are fixed on the true riches which is the whole end of the better covenant.

There is overwhelming evidence to show that wealth can blind man's eyes to reality. Underscoring this is Paul's counsel to Timothy about false teachers:

> *Perverse disputings of men of corrupt minds, and destitute of the truth, supposing that gain is godliness: from such withdraw thyself. But godliness with contentment is great gain. For we brought nothing into*

> *this world, and it is certain we can carry nothing out. And having food and raiment let us be therewith content. But they that will be rich fall into temptation and a snare, and into many foolish and hurtful lusts, which drown men in destruction and perdition. For the love of money is the root of all evil: which while some coveted after, they have erred from their faith, and pierced themselves through with many sorrows. But thou, O man of God, flee these things...*
>
> (1 Tim. 6:5-11).

Hence, economic status has little to do with the measure of God's blessing a person may or may not enjoy. One can be wealthy and greatly blessed of God, while another may be wealthy and totally devoid of God's blessing. Another may be poverty-stricken and yet mightily blessed of God. *Hearken, my beloved brethren, Hath not God chosen the poor of this world rich in faith, and heirs of the kingdom which he hath promised to them that love him?* (James 2:5). And yet a person can be poor and totally bereft of God's blessing.

Therefore let it be understood that God's blessings upon people are not dictated by economics, but by attitudes.

What then did Jesus mean when He said, *Blessed are the poor in spirit?*

Some of the modern translations of the New Testament can help us. Don Brankel, a well-known evangelist, was greatly exercised early in his ministry in an effort to find an answer to that question. Thinking his superior officer in the ministry could surely help him, he placed the question before him, only to discover that he too was pondering the same question. He then earnestly entreated the Lord for understanding, and almost immediately got his answer.

It came in a rather unusual way. While perusing the mail that had arrived on his desk, he was attracted to a flier advertising a new translation of the Bible . Printed in bold letters on the cover was an example of the translation which read: *The spiritually prosperous are the destitute and helpless* (Matt. 5:3). [2] He was assured he had the answer, especially when he found confirmation in Psalms 102:17: *He will regard the prayer of the destitute, and not despise their prayer.*

Destitution has a way of qualifying people for God's blessings. It is quite the opposite of self-sufficiency and human ingenuity which tend to deny any need for dependency upon God. These latter attributes are really a slap in God's face.

Everyone who would walk with God must learn that the first step toward His blessing is recognition of his own utter destitution, and admission of his own need. How often have the godly found that God has met them when they have exhausted all human means and have then cried unto Him.

Psalm 107 is a psalm of the destitute that illustrates this important point. Four times in that single psalm David cites Israel's destitution as the harbinger to God's intervention and ultimate blessing. We would do well to ponder his observations.

> *They wandered in the wilderness in a solitary way; they found no city to dwell in. Hungry and thirsty, their soul fainted in them. Then they cried unto the Lord in their trouble, and he delivered them out of their distresses. And he led them forth by the right way, that they might go to a city of habitation. Oh that men would praise the Lord for his goodness, and for his wonderful works to the children of men! For*

he satisfieth the longing soul, and filleth the hungry soul with goodness. Such as sit in darkness and in the shadow of death, being bound in affliction and iron; because they rebelled against the words of God, and contemned the counsel of the most High; therefore he brought down their heart with labour; they fell down, and there was none to help. Then they cried unto the Lord in their trouble, and he saved them out of their distresses. He brought them out of darkness and the shadow of death, and brake their bands in sunder. Oh that men would praise the Lord for his goodness, and for his wonderful works to the children of men! For he hath broken the gates of brass, and cut the bars of iron in sunder. Fools because of their transgression, and because of their iniquities, are afflicted. Their soul abhorreth all manner of meat; and they draw near unto the gates of death. Then they cry unto the Lord in their trouble, and he saveth them out of their distresses. He sent his word, and healed them, and delivered them from their destructions. Oh that men would praise the Lord for his goodness, and for his wonderful works to the children of men! And let them sacrifice the sacrifices of thanksgiving, and declare his works with rejoicing. They that go down to the sea in ships, that do business in great waters; these see the works of the Lord, and his wonders in the deep. For he commandeth, and raiseth the stormy wind, which lifteth up the waves thereof. They mount up to the heaven, they go down again to the depths: their soul is melted because of trouble. They reel to and fro, and stagger like a drunken man, and are at their wits' end. Then they cry unto the Lord in their trouble, and he bringeth them out of their distresses. He maketh the storm a calm, so that the waves thereof are still. Then are they glad because they be quiet; so he bringeth them unto their desired haven. Oh that men would praise the Lord for his goodness, and for his wonderful works to the children of men!

(Psa. 107:4-31)

Berkeley's version of the New Testament provides another insight: *Blessed are they who know their own spiritual poverty.*

The Delphic oracle in ancient Greece said, "Know thyself." Yet it is most difficult for unregenerate man to comprehend his own spiritual poverty, and to acknowledge his own spiritual condition and need. Paul described the lost as those: *In whom the god of this world hath blinded the minds of them which believe not, lest the light of the glorious gospel of Christ, who is the image of God, should shine unto them* (2 Cor. 4:4).

Even the believer can be robbed of God's blessings, being victimized by the Laodicean attitude: *Thou sayest, I am rich, and increased with goods, and have need of nothing; and knowest not that thou art wretched, and miserable, and poor, and blind, and naked* (Rev. 3:17).

While the believer is not to grovel in the dust of self-deprecation, he also must not permit self-deception about his true spiritual state, nor the luxury of an inflated opinion of himself to undermine the very foundations for his being blessed of God. *For I say, through the grace given unto me, to every man that is among you, not to think of himself more highly than he ought to think; but to think soberly, according as God hath dealt to every man the measure of faith* (Rom. 12:3). *Examine yourselves, whether ye be in the faith; prove your own selves* ...(2 Cor. 13:5).

It is not "child's play" at the present time to be poor in spirit. Almost all of modern society and our culture stands diametrically against it. This is a day of self-exaltation, a day of intense activity aimed at image improvement, a day of overmuch emphasis on positive thought, a day when the spirit of the world rides high, infecting even the family of God. The believer is told he is a "King's kid," and that he ought to claim all that is purportedly his right and privilege.

Furthermore, the case for sin has been dismissed. The idea that sin is the ultimate poverty is foreign to the modern mind.

But the truly poor in spirit are the people who have faced reality squarely. Such a person has discovered his own sinful bent and acts, and has shamefully admitted to his moral and spiritual bankruptcy.

It has been declared that the greatest discovery in mathematics is the zero. Someone once observed that the ultimate nothingness is a 0 (zero) without a rim. In the realm of the spiritual it is those who discover their own nothingness who also discover the greatest blessedness.

An example of being poor in spirit is Isaiah crying, *Woe is me! for I am undone; because I am a man of unclean lips, and I dwell in the midst of a people of unclean lips: for mine eyes have seen the King, the Lord of hosts* (Isa. 6:5). The poor in spirit is also the Publican smiting his breast and pleading, *God be merciful to me a sinner* (Luke 18:13). He is the smitten Paul on the Damascus Road praying, *Lord, what wilt thou have me to do?* (Acts 9:6). He is the anguished Peter who, after discovering his real self, went out and wept bitterly. He is a distraught Daniel travailing over his people in Israel:

> *And I set my face unto the Lord God, to seek by prayer and supplications, with fasting, and sackcloth, and ashes: and I prayed unto the Lord my God, and made my*

confession, and said, O Lord, the great and dreadful God, keeping the covenant and mercy to them that love him, and to them that keep his commandments; we have sinned, and have committed iniquity, and have done wickedly, and have rebelled, even by departing from thy precepts and from thy judgments: Neither have we hearkened unto thy servants the prophets, which spake in thy name to our kings, our princes, and our fathers, and to all the people of the land....

And he hath confirmed his words, which he spake against us, and against our judges that judged us, by bringing upon us a great evil: for under the whole heaven hath not been done as hath been done upon Jerusalem. As it is written in the law of Moses, all this evil is come upon us: yet made we not our prayer before the Lord our God, that we might turn from our iniquities, and understand thy truth. Therefore hath the Lord watched upon the evil, and brought it upon us: for the Lord our God is righteous in all his works which he doeth: for we obeyed not his voice. And now, O Lord our God, that hast brought thy people forth out of the land of Egypt with a mighty hand, and hast gotten thee renown, as at this day; we have sinned, we have done wickedly. O Lord, according to all thy righteousness, I beseech thee, let thine anger and thy fury be turned away from thy city Jerusalem, thy holy mountain: because for our sins, and for the iniquities of our fathers, Jerusalem and thy people are become a reproach to all that are about us. Now therefore, O our God, hear the prayer of thy servant, and his supplications, and cause thy face to shine upon thy sanctuary that is desolate, for the Lord's sake. O my God, incline thine ear, and hear; open thine eyes, and behold our desola-

tions, and the city which is called by thy name: for we do not present our supplications before thee for our righteousness, but for thy great mercies. O Lord, hear; O Lord, forgive; O Lord, hearken and do; defer not, for thine own sake, O my God: for thy city and thy people are called by thy name.

(Dan. 9:3-6 and 12-19)

"He" is any man coming to the Lord "humble-minded" (Phillips), "destitute and helpless in the realm of the spirit" (New English Bible), who "feel(s) poor in the realm of the spirit" (The Gospels, An Expanded Translation), "who feel(s) poor in spiritual thing(s)" (Williams), who is "humble, rating themselves (himself) insignificant" (Amplified), "who know(s) their (his) spiritual poverty" (Berkeley).

To this man belongs the Kingdom of heaven. He does not need to pursue it. It is his. He has qualified himself, and the Lord's blessing is his. He does not need to wait for eternity to obtain his dividend. The Kingdom of heaven is his now.

What then is this bounty of his — the Kingdom of heaven? Is it physical, earthly, tangible, visible? Luke indicates it is at least to some degree synonymous with the Kingdom of God when he states the Beatitude, *Blessed be ye poor: for yours is the kingdom of God.*

While some scholars perceive some difference between the Kingdom of heaven and the Kingdom of God, this is not the place to debate the issue. Suffice it to say, if we can discover the characteristics of one, we are also on track for the characteristics of the other.

Paul's ever keen insight unlocks the mystery. To the Romans he wrote, *For the kingdom of God is not meat and drink; but righteousness, and peace, and joy in the Holy Ghost*

(Rom. 14:17). It is not something for the natural appetite, such as meat and drink are. It is not to satisfy the lust of the flesh, such as material possessions and earthly wealth may do. It has no appeal to lusting eyes, for it is not visible and temporal.

But it is *righteousness.* It is Christ's righteousness freely bestowed upon the poor in spirit, in exchange for the filthy garments of their own totally inadequate self-righteousness.

It is *peace.* It is the peace for which all men seek, but so few find because it comes only to the poor in spirit. Upon them comes the Kingdom — first righteousness; then peace. *And the work of righteousness shall be peace; and the effect of righteousness quietness and assurance forever* (Isa. 32:17).

This peace has but a single source. Jesus said, *Peace I leave with you, my peace I give unto you: not as the world giveth, give I unto you ...*(John 14:27). It is both peace *with* God and the peace *of* God.

It is *joy.* It is heaven's joy. It is that joy which is native to God. *In thy presence is fullness of joy* (Psa. 16:11). It is the joy of fellowship with the Father. *That which we have seen and heard declare we unto you, that ye also may have fellowship with us: and truly our fellowship is with the Father, and with his Son Jesus Christ. And these things write we unto you, that your joy may be full* (1 John 1:3-4).

The poor in spirit receive the Kingdom which is the answer to all of man's deepest yearnings — righteousness in exchange for an ever-present sense of guilt; peace with God and the peace of God in place of a deep-seated sense of enmity and alienation; and the joy of His presence and fellowship to replace an innate sense of far-offness and loneliness.

Blessed are the poor in spirit, for theirs is the kingdom of heaven.

2

Good Grief

Blessed are they that mourn: for they shall be comforted (Matt. 5:4).

How blessed are the sorrowful (NEB). It sounds like a complete contradiction, like overblown positive thinking. How can sorrow or grief and blessing be in any way compatible? We think to be sorrowful is to be unblessed, and to be blessed is to escape sorrow.

Before pursuing an understanding of our Lord's intent in this second Beatitude, consider again the shades of meaning encompassed in the word "blessed" — to be blessed of God; to be in a state to be desired; being filled with life, joy and satisfaction; being enviably fortunate; being well-off and spiritually prosperous. How can any or all of these tantalizing prospects relate to all those who mourn?

The fact is, they don't! They relate only to a certain kind of mourning.

While God makes a balm available for all who mourn, Jesus was evidently addressing a form of mourning quite different from the kinds of mourning common to men.

God is identified by Paul as "the God of all comfort," and while Jesus is addressing a wholly different issue in this Beatitude, it must not go unnoted that God provides a special comfort for the mourning believer.

I learned this to my everlasting benefit when my father died. Only weeks before his sudden death at age eighty, I had visited him. He was the picture of health and was excitedly planning another of his life-long delights, a Canadian fishing trip.

Then suddenly the shocking news that he was dead came. My wife and I boarded the train en route from Montana to North Dakota for the funeral. My brothers and sister transported us from the railroad depot, some miles from my hometown. En route, they requested that I give a tribute to dad at the funeral. My reply was, "I'm not sure I can do it. After all, he was my own flesh and blood."

When we arrived at the mortuary, we saw his body lying in the casket and an overwhelming wave of grief swept over my soul. It lingered for only a passing moment. Before long, however, a wave of another kind washed over me — it was a quickening to my spirit of what I had so often preached, that what I was beholding in the casket was not dad at all. It was only the old tent he had inhabited for eighty years. He was not there. He had moved out, and was at that very moment present with the Lord.

My mourning was ended. God had indeed comforted my soul, and I was enabled to give the requested tribute without a problem. Nevertheless, there are many who mourn without comfort. Grief seems to intrude upon all humans like vultures upon a carcass. Everybody attempts to escape sorrow, grief and mourning. Adam Clarke insightfully notes "Everyone flies from sorrow and seeks after joy, and yet true joy must necessarily be the fruit of sorrow." [3]

Sorrow can have its own dividends, and often it does, for it seasons the soul and equips it for alleviating the heavy load borne by others. But there is a sorrow, a kind of mourning and grief, which in no way invites the blessing of God. It is identified in the Scriptures as: "the sorrow of the world." *For godly sorrow worketh repentance to salvation not to be repented of: but the sorrow of the world worketh death* (2 Cor. 7:10).

The Pulpit Commentary, speaking of the sorrow of the world, says,

> It works death. It wears the mind, sours the temper, fills the breast with discontent, takes away the zeal of exertion, chokes the heart with resentment and chagrin. It actually kills; a rankling annoyance or shame tends to both embitter and to shorten life. There are more than is commonly believed dying of vexation. [4]

Judas had the sorrow of the world, and it destroyed him. Most certainly it brought no blessing to him. His grief and mourning were for naught.

> *Then Judas, which had betrayed him, when he saw that he was condemned, repented himself, and brought again the thirty pieces of silver to the chief priests and elders, saying, I have sinned in that I have betrayed the innocent blood. And they said, What is that to us? see thou to that. And he cast down the pieces of silver in the temple, and departed, and went and hanged himself.*
>
> (Matt. 27:3-5)

Another, the rich young ruler, faced with the issues of life, experienced grief, not to any personal benefit, but to his eternal loss. His mourning led him to no blessedness.

> *Then Jesus beholding him loved him, and said unto him, one thing thou lackest: go thy way, sell whatsoever thou hast, and give to the poor, and thou shalt have treasure in heaven: and come, take up the cross, and follow me. And he was sad at that saying, and went away grieved: for he had great possessions.*
>
> (Mark 10: 21-22)

What then is that mourning, that sorrow, that grief which leads to blessedness? Here is the place to discover the vital relation of the Beatitudes to each other, and to understand that they are best interpreted in the light of their interrelationships. Therefore, when it is perceived that in the first Beatitude Jesus was zeroing in on the need for an attitude of destitution and poverty of spirit, it becomes readily perceivable also that in His second Beatitude He was targeting that attitude which naturally flows out of the first. That is the attitude of grieving and sorrow and mourning over a now recognized and owned-up-to state of spiritual poverty and destitution.

Mourning is the God-intended fruit of destitution. It is the God-expected and God-designed consequence of admitted poverty of spirit. God's order is: first, recognition of condition, followed by mourning over that condition. In other words, it is discovery, then recovery.

Until there is awareness of hindering attitudes which forestall God's blessing, correction of those attitudes is unlikely. Our problem is our own inflated view of our spiritual stature, our crediting ourselves with more than we have in the bank. There is a bit of Muhammad Ali's "I'm the greatest" in all of us.

Peter and his fellows were prime examples of this, and Peter, as was usually the case, verbalized it most loudly.

> *Then saith Jesus unto them, All ye shall be offended because of me this night: for it is written, I will smite the shepherd, and the sheep of the flock shall be scattered abroad. But after I am risen again, I will go before you into Galilee. Peter answered and said unto him, Though all men shall be offended because of thee, yet will I never be offended. Jesus said unto him, Verily I say unto thee, That this night, before the cock crow, thou shalt deny me thrice. Peter said unto him, Though I should die with thee, yet will I not deny thee. Likewise also said all the disciples.*
>
> (Matt: 26:31-35)

Even so, God is bent on blessing us, and He employs the necessary circumstances to awaken us to our true selves.

> *Now Peter sat without in the palace: and a damsel came unto him, saying, Thou also wast with Jesus of Galilee. But he denied before them all, saying, I know not what thou sayest. And when he was gone out into the porch, another maid saw him, and said unto them that were there, This fellow was also with Jesus of Nazareth. And again he denied with an oath, I do not know this man. And after a while came unto him they that stood by, and said to Peter, Surely thou also art one of them; for thy speech betrayeth thee. Then began he to curse and to swear, saying, I know not the*

man. And immediately the cock crew. And Peter remembered the word of Jesus, which said unto him, Before the cock crow, thou shalt deny me thrice...."
(Matt. 26:69-75)

What a profound contrast there can be between who we think we are, how loudly we profess our fidelity, *Though I should die with thee, yet will I not deny thee,* and who we really are when the heat is applied: *Then began he to curse and to swear* (that is, to invite a curse upon himself, and to swear, as before a court of law), *saying, I know not the man!*

It had to happen to awaken Peter. The crowing of a cock turned the trick. Suddenly Peter saw himself, his poverty, his destitution and he mourned: *And he went out, and wept bitterly* (Matt. 26:75). His grief was good and genuine. It was the sorrow of unfeigned repentance.

And it paved the way for his being blessed. His attitude had been sharply altered, and he was comforted, even by an angel with a special message. *But go your way, tell his disciples and Peter* (not that Peter was not any longer a disciple, but rather especially Peter who was mourning over his true self so deeply) *that he goeth before you into Galilee: there shall ye see him, as he said unto you* (Mark 16:7).

What wondrous comfort for the destitute!

And what of the crowd that assembled outside the upper room on the Day of Pentecost? They had participated in the Crucifixion of our Lord. In all likelihood, they had done so without a tinge of conscience. They were the religious of the day. They did not fall short in observing the Jewish rites and ceremonies. That is what brought many of them to Jerusalem. They were the "children of Abraham." They were God's chosen people.

Nevertheless they were blind, but they thought they saw. *For had they known it, they would not have crucified the Lord of glory* (1 Cor. 2:8).

Not until Peter, mightily moved upon and carried along by the Holy Spirit, bore down on them, did they awaken to their blindness and their utter spiritual destitution. His scathing denunciation was the sharp sword that cut through the shroud of their religiosity and invaded their true selves.

> *Ye men of Israel, hear these words; Jesus of Nazareth, a man approved of God among you by miracles and wonders and signs, which God did by him in the midst of you, as ye yourselves also know; him, being delivered by the determinate counsel and foreknowledge of God, ye have taken, and by wicked hands have crucified and slain.*
>
> (Acts 2:22-23)

Only then did they look upon Him whom they had pierced, and only then, *...they were pricked in their heart, and said unto Peter and to the rest of the apostles, Men and brethren, what shall we do?* (Acts 2:37). Only then was born in them an attitude of mourning over their recognized spiritual poverty and only then did the prophecy of Zechariah find its first fulfillment.

> *And I will pour upon the house of David, and upon the inhabitants of Jerusalem, the spirit of grace and of supplications: and they shall look upon me whom they have pierced, and they shall mourn for him, as one mourneth for his only son, and shall be in bitterness for him, as one that is in bitterness for his firstborn. In that day shall there be a great mourning in Jerusa-*

lem, as the mourning of Hadadrimmon in the valley of Megiddon.

(Zech. 12:10-11)

While that prophecy, no doubt, anticipates events yet to come, those present were immediately awarded with God's comfort: *Then they that gladly received his word were baptized: and the same day there were added unto them about three thousand souls* (Acts 2:41).

Encompassed also in this second Beatitude is that attitude of grieving, mourning and sorrowing over the destitution and spiritual poverty of others. There is an unselfish occupation with their woeful condition which yields its own compensation and comfort.

It was thus that Moses was exercised over his people, Israel, when he lamented,

Ye have sinned a great sin: and now I will go up unto the Lord; peradventure I shall make an atonement for your sin. And Moses returned unto the Lord, and said, Oh, this people have sinned a great sin, and have made them gods of gold. Yet now, if thou wilt forgive their sin—; and if not, blot me, I pray thee, out of thy book which thou hast written.

(Exod. 32:30-32)

And who can overlook the unparalleled mourning of Jesus in His confronting the sins of the whole ungodly world? His own agonizing statement emanating from Gethsemane's dark shadows shows His attitude of mourning over sin: *My soul is exceeding sorrowful, even unto death* (Matt. 26:38). Surely Isaiah foresaw the blessedness of the comfort he experienced when he announced, *He shall see of the travail of his soul, and shall be satisfied...* (Isa. 53:11).

In a similar manner we see the Apostle Paul's mournful attitude over the state of his physical and spiritual kinsmen: *I say the truth in Christ, I lie not, my conscience also bearing me witness in the Holy Ghost, that I have great heaviness and continual sorrow in my heart. For I could wish that myself were accursed from Christ for my brethren, my kinsmen according to the flesh* (Rom. 9:1-3).

It comes through again in his letter to the Galatians: *My little children* (the Galatians) *of whom I travail in birth again until Christ be formed in you* (Gal. 4:19).

And it is after this same manner that we in the Church today are invited and challenged to stand alongside of Moses, Jesus and Paul, sharing in their mournful attitude over the prevailing spiritual climate, and ultimately in that blessedness springing from such vicarious identification.

For the Church, there is the further need for an attitude of mourning over her own destitution, her spiritual poverty, her deafness and deadness, her blindness, her humanism, her inability to discern between truth and error, her bent toward materialism, her occupation with fads and fancies, her prayerlessness, over her doctrinal deviation and over her inability to discern spiritual reality.

Over the perishing world, too, there is reason for an attitude of mourning, for they know not God and obey not the gospel. *Awake to righteousness, and sin not; for some have not the knowledge of God: I speak this to your shame* (1 Cor. 15:34).

What exciting dividends await those who espouse such compassionate and worthy attitudes over their own destitution, and over the destitution of others. *To appoint unto them that mourn in Zion, to give unto them beauty for ashes, the oil of joy for mourning, the garment of praise for the spirit of heaviness; that they might be called trees of righteousness, the planting of the Lord, that he might be glorified* (Isa. 61:3).

Incredible blessedness awaits the mourner. In exchange for his "ashes" — what could be more valueless — he is comforted with the beauty of God's holiness. In exchange for his mourning, he is comforted with the oil of joy. In exchange for his annoying and consuming spirit of heaviness, he is comforted with the garment of praise. And add to all of this the prospect of being called *trees of righteousness, the planting of the Lord, that he might be glorified.*

Blessed are they that mourn: for they shall be comforted!

3

On Inheriting the Earth

Blessed are the meek: for they shall inherit the earth (Matt. 5:5).

Oh, the blessedness of the poor in spirit!

Oh, the blessedness of those who mourn!

Oh, the blessedness of the meek!

There is a natural sequence in the organization of the Beatitudes. Apart from poverty of spirit, and apart from mourning over that acknowledged poverty, there generally will be little genuine meekness. Meekness flows out of an attitude of poverty of spirit, and the consequential attitude of mourning, as naturally as water flows from an artesian well. All that is required of man is that he make it possible.

So here we have the third vital thread in the Great Artist's tapestry — the attitude of meekness.

Meekness is a greatly-to-be-coveted posture of the soul. "Meekness," says *The Pulpit Commentary,*

> is the attitude of the soul towards another when that other is in a state of activity towards it. It is the attitude of the disciple to the teacher when teaching; of the son to the father when exercising his paternal authority; of the servant to the master when giving him orders.... It is an inwrought grace of the soul; and the exercises of it are first and chiefly towards God (Matt. 11:19; Jas.1:21). It is the temper of the spirit in which we accept His dealings with us as good, and therefore without disputing or resisting ...it is only the humble heart which is also the meek; and which as such, does not fight against God, and more or less struggle and contend with Him. Yet, as this meekness must be felt towards God not only in His direct dealings with the soul, but also in His indirect dealings (i.e. by secondary means and agents), it must also be exhibited toward men. Meekness towards God necessarily issues in meekness towards men. [5]

A. W. Tozer wrote,

> The meek man is not a human mouse, afflicted with a sense of his own inferiority. Rather he may be in his own moral life, as bold as a lion and as strong as Samson, but he has stopped being fooled about himself. He has accepted God's estimate of his own life. He knows he is weak and helpless as God has declared him to be, but paradoxically, he knows at the same time that he is in the sight of God of more importance than angels. In himself nothing; in God everything. [6]

An attitude of godly meekness is not easily acquired as is loudly proclaimed by the fact that only two individuals in all the Bible are credited with being meek, one in the Old Testament —the incomparable lawgiver, Moses — and one in the New Testament — none less than Jesus, our Lord.

In order to discover the qualities of meekness and the means for obtaining them, it is for us to take a look at the lives of those who assuredly possessed meekness.

The Scriptures say of Moses, *Now the man Moses was very meek, above all the men which were upon the face of the earth* (Num. 12:3). These lines shine like bright lights in thick darkness, portraying Moses as a brilliant diamond against a backdrop of blackness.

Three characters constitute the cast for the drama: Moses, the "baby brother" (aged eighty-one), Aaron his older brother (aged eighty-four) and Miriam, their only sister who was older than both of them. It is a family affair. Moses is the God-appointed leader for all of Israel. Aaron is the high priest, the minister of religion, and Miriam is the prophetess and the director of music. *And Miriam the prophetess, the sister of Aaron, took a timbrel in her hand; and all the women went out after her with timbrels and with dances. And Miriam answered them, Sing ye to the Lord, for he hath triumphed gloriously; the horse and his rider hath he thrown into the sea* (Exod. 15:20-21).

It cannot be denied that in both Testaments family relationships among those in leadership roles were frequently cited among God's people. Before us is a classic Old Testament example: Moses, Aaron and Miriam, all of one family. And in the New Testament similar examples are easily found: Elisabeth and Mary, Jesus' mother, were first cousins, while Jesus and John the Baptist were second cousins. Also in the band of Jesus' twelve disciples there were at least two brothers, James and John. Other examples could be cited as well. Even so, while the Scriptures do not forbid it, there is evidence and some personal experience that indicates that when church leadership becomes too much of a family affair, built-in pitfalls may cause problems. Having more than one member from the same family on a church board, for example, unless great care and godly integrity are present, can become a source of sharp contention that leads to severe disruption and division. The same can be the case when too many members of the pastor's immediate family are on his staff. Admittedly there are advantages to such an arrangement; yet the inherent dangers tend to outweigh the advantages. Blood, as has been said, runs thicker than water. Partiality toward our own is not easily avoided, and the resulting congregational displeasure is too easily generated.

Moses' family affair ought to give us a fair warning. Jealousy and subtle desire for more recognition and authority all too easily creep in. Human nature insists on equal rights, which, incidentally, has become an annoying and troublesome problem in our generation. We are confronted with rights issues almost daily — women's rights, children's rights, citizen's rights, social rights, Indian rights, black rights, white rights, minority rights, political rights, conventional rights, gay rights, educational rights, spotted-owl rights, animal rights, individual rights. The list is unending; yet all the while, as with Aaron and Miriam, the inclination is to overlook Him who has <u>first</u> rights and <u>all</u> rights.

Aaron and Miriam conceived the idea that they ought to have equal rights with Moses, overlooking the fact that God himself had appointed Moses to Israel's leadership. But they used a subtle ploy to camouflage their secret ambitions. *And Miriam and Aaron spake against Moses because of the Ethiopian woman whom he had married....And they said, Hath the Lord indeed spoken only by Moses? hath he not spoken also by us? And the Lord heard it* (Num. 12:1-2). They would cover up their ungodly intent to lower Moses' status and to raise their own by dredging out of the past a long-harbored bit of ill will over their brother's marriage to a woman who was not of their liking. Who she was is not clear. It is possible the reference is to Zipporah whom he married while a fugitive from justice on the backside of the desert. If so, he had been married to her for some forty-one years, from about 1531 B.C. to 1490 B.C. Or the reference could have been to a second woman whom Moses married who was possibly a Cashite of Hamitic origin and perhaps black.

Who she was, however, is of little consequence. Making her the focus of their accusation was simply a subtle ploy for justifying their sedition. They wanted at least equal rights with Moses, and for them the end justified the means.

Whether Moses heard their complaint we do not know. But God did! *And the Lord heard it.* What a sobering thought — God knows our attitudes and our actions!

The meek do not need to defend themselves. The Lord defends them. The inheritance is theirs without fighting for it. *Blessed are the meek: for they shall inherit the earth.*

Suddenly the Lord came upon the scene:

> *And the Lord spake suddenly unto Moses, and unto Aaron, and unto Miriam, Come out ye three unto the tabernacle of the congregation. And they three came out. And the Lord came down in the pillar of the*

> *cloud, and stood in the door of the tabernacle, and called Aaron and Miriam: and they both came forth. And he said, Hear now my words: if there be a prophet among you, I the Lord will make myself known unto him in a vision, and will speak unto him in a dream. My servant Moses is not so, who is faithful in all mine house. With him will I speak mouth to mouth, even apparently, and not in dark speeches; and the similitude of the Lord shall he behold: wherefore then were ye not afraid to speak against my servant Moses? And the anger of the Lord was kindled against them; and he departed. And the cloud departed from off the tabernacle; and, behold, Miriam became leprous, white as snow: and Aaron looked upon Miriam, and, behold, she was leprous. And Aaron said unto Moses, Alas, my lord, I beseech thee, lay not the sin upon us, wherein we have done foolishly, and wherein we have sinned. Let her not be as one dead, of whom the flesh is half consumed when he cometh out of his mother's womb. And Moses cried unto the Lord, saying, Heal her now, O God, I beseech thee. And the Lord said unto Moses, If her father had but spit in her face, should she not be ashamed seven days? Let her be shut out from the camp seven days, and after that let her be received in again. And Miriam was shut out from the camp seven days: and the people journeyed not till Miriam was brought in again.*
>
> (Num. 12:4-15)

Even in the midst of this awful scene, Moses' meekness shines through. If it were not for his attitude of unpretended meekness, he would likely have said, in the face of Miriam's judgment, "Lay it on her, Lord, she deserves it. After all, look how she treated poor me. Shut her out!"

But it was not so. Instead Moses pled with all his might that his sister might not be shut out of the camp. No wonder Jesus said, *Blessed are the meek!*

By his own testimony, Jesus was meek: *Come unto me, all ye that labour and are heavy laden, and I will give you rest. Take my yoke upon you, and learn of me; for I am meek and lowly in heart: and ye shall find rest unto your souls. For my yoke is easy, and my burden is light* (Matt. 11:28-30).

And Paul attests to that inherent meekness in Jesus when he says, *Now I Paul myself beseech you by the meekness and gentleness of Christ...* (2 Cor. 10:1).

Ultimately, meekness is wholehearted submission to proper authority. Remember, "Meekness is the attitude of the soul towards another when the other is in a state of activity toward it...the attitude of the servant to the master when giving him orders...of the son to the father when exercising his paternal authority."

Thus, meekness for the child of God is best reflected in unquestioning submission to the Father's will. It is epitomized in Jesus' statement, *I do always those things that please him* (the Father) (John 8:29).

Meekness is the cornerstone of the believer's authority. *And they were astonished at his doctrine: for he taught them as one that had authority, and not as the scribes* (Mark 1:22). In every area of Christian life and ministry, the degree of authority one may hold is never meant to be greater than the degree of meekness or the degree of submission in that individual's life.

In vain do men seek to exercise authority over Satan, over sickness and over circumstances, if they have not learned first the ABC's of meekness and submission. But let a man learn meekness, and authority automatically becomes his. He is as bold as a lion. He does not have to pretend. *Submit yourselves therefore to God. Resist the devil, and he will flee from you* (James 4:7).

How does the attitude of meekness become part of a person's nature? Surely it is not inherent in human nature. It is not a cheaply bought commodity. It is not a product of genetic engineering, nor is it acquired by mere human resolution.

It is a characteristic of the divine nature, and thus it comes to those who partake of God's nature. It is available to those who seek Him and His nature. *Seek ye the Lord, all ye meek of the earth, which have wrought his judgment; seek righteousness, seek meekness...* (Zeph. 2:3). Meekness bears its own reward. *They shall inherit the earth.* They need not pursue blessedness. It is theirs.

But what constitutes inheriting the earth? Is this a futuristic pledge to the meek that relates to the Millennium? Does it somehow connect to the promise given to Abraham in Genesis 13:14-17?

> *And the Lord said unto Abram, after that Lot was separated from him, Lift us now thine eyes, and look from the place where thou art northward, and southward, and eastward, and westward: for all the land which thou seest, to thee will I give it, and to thy seed for ever. And I will make thy seed as the dust of the earth: so that if a man can number the dust of the earth, then shall thy seed also be numbered. Arise, walk through the land in the length of it and in the breadth of it; for I will give it unto thee.*

Undoubtedly our Lord's intent was to declare the highest Christian principle, that the meek who minister and serve, who are ever ready to consider themselves the least, while pursuing the highest good of others, are those who in the end receive the highest honor, the chiefest place and the most royal, and enduring empire. They inherit much more than *terra firma*.. Theirs is "the life that now is," with the added blessing of ...*houses, and brethren, and sisters, and mothers, and children, and lands* (Mark 10:30).

Theirs also is the blessing of which the Canaan promised to Abraham was but a shadow — the infilling with the Holy Spirit who is declared to be the earnest to the saints' inheritance. *That the blessing of Abraham might come on the Gentiles through Jesus Christ; that we might receive the promise of the Spirit through faith* (Gal. 3:14).

In whom ye also trusted, after that ye heard the word of truth, the gospel of your salvation: in whom also after that ye believed, ye were sealed with that holy Spirit of promise, which is the earnest of our inheritance until the redemption of the purchased possession, unto the praise of his glory (Eph. 1:13-14).

Add to all of that the further dividends that are afforded to the meek, and you must conclude that the attitude of meekness is a jewel worthy of our earnest pursuit.

The meek shall eat and be satisfied: they shall praise the Lord that seek him: your heart shall live for ever (Psa. 22:26).

The meek will he guide in judgment: and the meek will he teach his way (Psa. 25:19).

But the meek shall inherit the earth; and shall delight themselves in the abundance of peace (Psa. 37:11).

The Lord lifteth up the meek: he casteth the wicked down to the ground (Psa. 147:6).

For the Lord taketh pleasure in his people: he will beautify the meek with salvation (Psa. 149:4).

The meek also shall increase their joy in the Lord, and the poor among men shall rejoice in the Holy One of Israel (Isa. 29:19).

Blessed are the meek, for they shall inherit the earth.

4

"Fill My Cup, Lord"

Blessed are they which do hunger and thirst after righteousness: for they shall be filled (Matt. 5:6).

We come now to thread number four in the divine tapestry. It has already been established that certain specific attitudes build the highway on which God's blessings travel — that an attitude of poverty of spirit is rewarded with the Kingdom of heaven, that an attitude of grief and mourning over admitted poverty of spirit invites God's comfort, and that an attitude of meekness, springing from the foregoing attitudes, sets the stage for an incredible inheritance.

The succession is both natural and necessary, much as each succeeding step in a stairway is natural and necessary for reaching another level. Each acquired attitude creates the possibility of each succeeding attitude.

This being the case, there is a minimal likelihood of any degree of hunger and thirst after righteousness apart from an initial recognition of one's poverty of spirit, followed by mourning and grief over that condition and a subsequent resulting attitude of unfeigned meekness.

Hunger and thirst after righteousness are attitudes that are greatly to be valued and coveted, but they are alarmingly absent. The appetite for righteousness occupies the same house as spiritual health and wholeness in the same way that physical hunger and thirst dwell within the larger structure of physical well-being.

A while ago I took my two grandsons, Shane and Travis, on a fishing excursion to Canada. Our preparation for the first day's fishing included a substantial supply of sandwiches. After a few hours of being in the boat fishing we had our first round of sandwiches, leaving an ample supply for our noon lunch — or so we thought! However, when noon arrived, and we were ready to eat, we discovered, somewhat to our consternation, that no sandwiches remained. Travis, the younger of the two boys, had secretly devoured the whole lot. His reason? "Grandpa, I was hungry!"

On another occasion I visited an elderly minister in the hospital. He had been my pastor when I was a young man. His word to me was, "Bob, I have lost my appetite. I have no desire to eat." Not long afterwards, I was notified of his death and asked to conduct his funeral.

Much as there is a close proximity between health and hunger, there is also a close proximity between lack of appetite and death. Both food and water are absolute necessities for maintaining physical life and well being. Spiritual food and water are likewise essential components for spiritual growth and health.

Reportedly, a bird can survive nine days without food; turtles can survive for as long as 500 days without sustenance, and snakes can live for up to 800 days without a thing to eat.

What about man? Forty days is generally about his limit.

Some humans, for diverse reasons, practice extreme dieting habits, even to the point of deliberately regurgitating food they have eaten. This results in an eating disorder known as bulimia. Anorexia nervosa is another eating disorder in which an individual literally starves himself. In the anorexic, the willful denial of food generates a physical inability to consume food, a condition that is sometimes irreversible, ultimately resulting in death.

There is a spiritual counterpart to these physical conditions. When man, for whatever reason, whether he sees no value in it or whether he willfully rejects hungering and thirsting after righteousness, denies himself the means to God's blessedness, he invites spiritual emptiness and even disaster upon himself.

God does no force-feeding. He gives no intravenous injections. Even as this chapter is being written, the media is reporting a hunger strike in a South American state which has brought many participants to the brink of death over the cause of political prisoners held by the government. Authorities in charge are threatening to intravenously force-feed those strikers who are near death, entirely against the hunger strikers' wills.

Such tactics are never employed by God. He is dependent upon every man's hunger and thirst. His righteousness is never imposed. It is always imputed. However, He may employ prevailing circumstances to jump-start hunger and thirst for it. Such was the case with Israel. It may well be the case with us. *And he humbled thee, and suffered thee to hunger, and fed thee with manna, which thou knewest not, neither did thy fathers know; that he might make thee know that man doth not live by bread only, but by every word that proceedeth out of the mouth of the Lord doth man live* (Deut. 8:3).

The circumstances He employs may not be pleasant. Though God is never the instigator of evil, He does employ evil in His great passion for man's good. For example, the multiplied evils of men, foreknown by God, but never instigated by Him, which took His Son to the awful cross, culminated in a glorious outcome — the availability of salvation for all men (see Acts 2:22-24).

A spiritual drought can generate spiritual hunger and thirst. Historically, long-standing spiritual droughts have begotten spiritual hunger and thirst, which in turn have generated a kind of desperation for God which has not gone unrewarded.

Moral decay, social disintegration and spiritual disinterest invariably terminate in either of two ways. Either they produce their own antidote, like the body produces antibodies for overcoming life-threatening infections or disease, or, on the other hand, exterior forces, perhaps even divine vengeance, bring them to their destruction.

In the United States presently, evil is on a rampage. The moral conditions and climate of our land are worse than at any time in history. No longer does man blush over his sensual deviations. He has no desire or time for God. His imaginations are only evil continually. Righteousness, and the desire for it, are foreign to him. As in Lot's day, the souls of the righteous are vexed from day to day with the flood tide of evil (see 2 Peter 2:8).

Social disintegration abounds. Seemingly solid and wholesome family units break apart at alarming rates, and social disorder and dysfunction race across the land like a prairie fire. Mingled with all of this, and the fruit of it as well, is an evident and widespread distaste for godliness, and not uncommonly a vicious castigating and ridiculing of it.

Yet, a voice is crying in this wilderness, *Blessed are they which do hunger and thirst after righteousness; for they shall be filled!*

To those whose cups have been filled to overflowing with panting *after the dust of the earth* (Amos 2:7) and who are saturated to the limit with hewing out *cisterns, broken cisterns, that can hold no water* (Jer. 2:13), and who *sow much and bring in little; who eat, but have not enough, who drink and are not filled; who clothe themselves and are not warmed, and who earn wages to put them in bags with holes in them* (Hag. 1:6, author's paraphrase), the voice is crying:

> *Ho, everyone that thirsteth, come ye to the waters, and he that hath no money; come ye, buy, and eat; yea, come, buy wine and milk without money and without price. Wherefore do ye spend money for that which is not bread? And your labour for that which satisfieth not? Hearken diligently unto me, and eat ye that which is good, and let your soul delight itself in fatness.*
>
> (Isa. 55:1-2)

For the truly hungry and thirsty there is a glorious provision. The choice is possible. The alternatives are clear. It is either altered attitudes — admitted spiritual paupery, repentant mourning over that awful state, acquired meekness, accompanied by hunger and thirst after righteousness — or it is the inevitable serious consequences that end in judgment and destruction. There is little room for doubting those consequences.

But the latter need not be, nor does God wish it to be. He always wants the best for man and He is ready to bestow it. All He awaits and requires is the proper spiritual climate. Man's hungering and thirsting for righteousness is the lever for turning on the fullness of His blessing, and the pathway for escaping the meager existence of spiritual poverty into *the measure of the stature of the fulness of Christ* (Eph. 4:13).

I have observed that if man will but hunger and thirst, God will fill him; but that hunger and thirst must be for a proper sort of righteousness if he is to partake of the kind of filling God envisions for him.

That attitude of hunger and thirst for which God scans the whole earthly scene, and which is so easily substituted with desire for much lesser things, is for an absolutely singular thing which Jesus identifies as "righteousness."

What then is this righteousness which awaits our impassioned pursuit? Until men know, they will not pursue.

J. E. Phillips has translated Matthew 5:6 as follows: *Happy are those who are hungry and thirsty for goodness, for they will be fully satisfied.* The *New English Bible* puts it, *How blest are those who hunger and thirst to see right prevail; they shall be satisfied.*

Geoffrey W. Bromiley, in addressing and identifying the righteousness of Matthew 5:6, says, "The hungering and thirsting of 5:6 is for a right state before God. Yet this righteousness is God's Gift (6:33). It is to be sought with his kingdom." [7] *The Pulpit Commentary* identifies it as "...that right relation to God in which they were so lacking." Ultimately it is the righteousness of God, as contrasted with any supposed righteousness with which a man may credit himself.

It is imperative that this be understood, for no lesser righteousness can qualify for the dividend. There is a righteousness which is of the Law. It is the righteousness of good works, and it might be called the righteousness of Cain, which is purely and simply self-righteousness. It is the righteousness of the Scribes and Pharisees which Jesus declared must be exceeded in order to enter into the Kingdom of heaven (see Matt. 5:20). Commonly those who are its victims perceive little need for that righteousness addressed by Jesus, and thus they have little or no hunger and thirst for it. *For they being ignorant of God's righteousness, and going about to establish their own righteousness, have not submitted themselves unto the righteousness of God* (Rom. 10:3).

Man's own righteousness as compared with God's is the difference between a silk rose perfumed with a concocted scent, and a real rose emanating its own inimitable and glorious fragrance. Only those who recognize the utter folly and worthlessness of their own brand of righteousness will hunger and thirst for that righteousness which Jesus envisioned.

Indeed, the righteousness which is awaiting the hunger and thirst of man is beyond the reach of man. No man has ever acquired it by his most valiant human effort. He may have gotten a glimpse of it through the Law. Yet, when he, with all his human might, has pursued it by his efforts to keep the Law or by any other means, like a mirage in the burning desert, it has escaped him.

The fact that it is beyond his reach may well be God's means of generating his hunger and thirst for it, and of setting the stage for his receiving it.

So long as man, by his own measurement, has an adequate righteousness, he recognizes no need for another kind of righteousness; but when the Law of God and the Spirit of God combine to awaken him, suddenly his supposed righteousness becomes like despicable garbage to him, and he cries with Paul, *O wretched man that I am!*

(Rom. 7:24). *Wherefore the law was our schoolmaster to bring us unto Christ* (Gal. 3:24).

Thus we conclude that the righteousness envisioned in this Beatitude was a kind all its own. It is, as we have said, the righteousness of God himself. It is a singular kind of righteousness which will permit no counterfeit or substitute. It is the only righteousness which can withstand the blazing heat of God's holiness. Every other form of righteousness is like straw before the furnace.

Howbeit, this righteousness of God can be man's, but only when he stands empty-handed before God, acknowledging the utter worthlessness of any vestige of righteousness he may have clung to and leaned upon for admission into God's Kingdom. He can't earn it. He can't buy it. He can't bargain for it. Yet, all he needs is the proper attitude, and it becomes his — the attitude of genuine hunger and thirst for it.

Earlier in this chapter we stated, "Each acquired attitude created the possibility of each succeeding attitude." My father, when a fourteen-year-old young man, migrated to the United States from Germany. Although he had a bit of a formal church background, he was little interested in "that sort of religion." As he grew older, he and his brothers were dubbed "the roughnecks on the hill." But he had a praying mother.

In due time he married and became a farmer in his own right. He seldom, if ever, attended a church. Sunday was for greasing his Model-T Ford, and for doing chores around the farmyard.

He smoked a pipe until his teeth were worn down. He danced the polka with the neighbors until the house shook, and he lived the life of a worldling.

On an occasion his barn burned, and thinking the ashes from his pipe had caused it, he threw the pipe, tobacco and matches into the fire, swearing he would never smoke again. Mother said it lasted three days, and she could hardly live with him. So he started over again. He said he figured if he had to choose between his wife and his pipe, he'd likely have to choose his pipe for he couldn't live without it!

But a neighbor dropped by one day to invite him to a meeting in a nearby consolidated country schoolhouse. The neighbor mentioned that a young preacher would be ministering.

Despite his feeling no need whatever for anything of a religious nature, he accepted the invitation for no other reason than to accommodate his farmer friend. He hadn't the slightest tinge of hunger or thirst for righteousness, for he thought of himself as a good and righteous man. If anyone was going to heaven, he was!

In the meeting that evening the young preacher addressed the question of salvation for young children. He seemed to go over the same material several times, until dad found himself disagreeing rather heartily. Finally he thought he had had enough. He decided that if the preacher repeated himself once more, he would get up and publicly disagree with him. And, knowing dad as I did, I don't doubt he would have done it — except for a strange turn of events.

As the preacher began again on the same course, dad was ready for him. Taking hold of the eighth-grade desk in which he sat, he was about to rise and make his challenge. But he never did. Instead, the preacher noted that dad turned white as a ghost and remained seated.

I have heard him recite many times what happened. He said that at the moment when he was about to stand, he suddenly had a most remarkable out-of-the-body experience. From near the ceiling of the schoolroom, he was looking down and seeing himself, not as a good and righteous man, but as the community's worst sinner. He was shocked literally speechless.

When the meeting ended, he hastened out, assuring himself, as he drove homeward that he would soon shake off this strange intrusion.

Thereafter he walked alone in his fields in the evenings, pondering what had happened, while within his being a gentle voice whispered, *If you will just bow your knee. If you will just bow your knee.* But he couldn't. His attitude was so rigid and fixed. How could he change?

Two long weeks passed and the struggle persisted. Over and over he kept hearing, *If you will just bow your knee.* To do it would be to admit his utter spiritual bankruptcy, and how could he, a good and righteous man, do that? But that inner voice was as relentless as a pack of hounds baying after their prey.

Finally it all came to a head in the middle of the third week. He broke. Kneeling over a rock in the field, he surrendered to a whole new set of attitudes. His kneeling, in one glorious act, announced to God and to the observing angels his now-admitted poverty of spirit, his deep mourning over his awful condition, his new-born meekness, which issued in his submission, and his very real and rising hunger and thirst for a righteousness far beyond his own.

And in that hour, God confirmed the blessed Beatitude to him, for he was almost instantly filled, not with his own self-righteousness, but with the righteousness of God himself.

En route home that evening he prayed for his wife (my mother) that she would have a similar experience. When he laid his head upon his pillow that very night, having told her nothing of his new-found experience, she arose, and for the first time in their married lives, knelt beside the bed, hardly realizing or understanding why she did it.

Within days the neighbors began to say, "Brandt's got religion," though he had not yet told anyone. Far more than religion, my father now had a relationship with Jesus Christ.

His whole life-style, like that of Saul of Tarsus, had undergone a radical change, reflecting that true righteousness which had been imputed to him. He began devouring God's Word. His solidly entrenched habits fell off like leaves from a frost-bitten tree. Never again did he smoke. His dancing the polka ceased. No longer did he gamble and take the name of his Lord in vain. Now, with all his might, he pursued Him whom his soul loved.

For over fifty years thereafter he walked with God until his decease; but not alone, for his entire family followed close behind him.

The pledge, *for they shall be filled,* predicts God's certain response to the acquired attitude. The attitude must be solely man's; the provision is solely God's. When man hungers and thirsts for God's righteousness, his hunger and thirst are satisfied with that righteousness. The filling is commensurate with the degree of hunger and thirst.

> St. Austin, wondering at the overflowing measure of God's Spirit in the Apostles' hearts, observes that the reason why they were so full of God was because they were so empty of his creatures. 'They were very full,' he says, 'because they were very empty.' That on earth, but in heaven with all the saints —

Ever filled and ever seeking,
What they have they still desire,
Hunger there shall fret them never,
Nor satiety shall tire, —
Still enjoying whilst aspiring,
In their joy they still aspire. [8]

The lone and exclusive Source of the filling is God. The single access is Jesus. He is the Mediator of the transaction. He is the means of its possibility. *For he* (God) *hath made him to be sin for us, who knew no sin; that we might be made the righteousness of God in him* (2 Cor. 5:21).

Yet the questions linger: How can it happen to the individual? How may the hungry and thirsty be filled? How can they be thus blessed? How can a man *...win Christ, and be found in him, not having mine own righteousness, which is of the law, but that which is through the faith of Christ, the righteousness which is of God by faith* (Phil. 3:8-9)?

The answer is plainly set forth in the Scriptures. Though God's righteousness is always a gift of His amazing grace, and though it is, and must ever be, an imputed righteousness, the track upon which it runs, and by which it reaches the hungry and thirsty is always and forever the same — *faith. For what saith the scripture? Abraham believed God, and it was counted unto him for righteousness* (Rom. 4:3). When man fixes his faith in Jesus for gaining God's righteousness, then and only then is He made unto us *...wisdom, and righteousness, and sanctification, and redemption* (1 Cor. 1:30).

Blessed are they which do hunger and thirst after righteousness, for they shall be filled.

Fill my cup, Lord.

5

Antidote for Judgment

Blessed are the merciful: for they shall obtain mercy (Matt. 5:7).

Oh, the blessedness of the merciful!

Thread number five in the Great Artist's tapestry is mercifulness — a special attitude that solicits God's special blessing.

Attitude number one relates to the state of our spirit; number two relates to our mourning over that recognized state of spirit; number three deals with the resultant meekness — that is, our submission to God and others; number four is concerned with our now-awakened inner longing and desire for righteousness; and number five relates to our treatment of others, especially as it relates to undeserved affliction and to judgment.

It is not likely that our treatment of others will measure up to God's expectation until the already-examined other four preparatory attitudes are found in us. All of these combining together, and culminating in true righteousness, prepare the seedbed for those yet to follow.

Of great importance is our understanding that mercy springs up like a flower from the properly cultivated seedbed of righteousness; or to state it in another way, righteousness yields a variety of fruits, including mercifulness.

At the outset we want to discover what Jesus had in mind by His use of the word "merciful." The English equivalent of the Greek word used for "merciful" is "compassionate." The Greek *eleemon* is translated "merciful or "sympathetic," and it is used mostly in relationship to God. In Hebrews 2:17 the word "merciful" describes Christ himself who praises the virtues of this attitude in the fifth Beatitude.

The Greek word *eleos* (also *pathos*) to which *eleemon* is closely related is

> ...the emotion aroused by undeserved affliction in others and containing an element of fear as well as mercy. It is wholly fitting in the noble, and plays a part in the administering of justice. For the Stoics, however, it is a sickness unworthy of the Sage, not because the Stoics are cruel, but because they do not think moral relations should be governed by a pathos. [9]

"Merciful" has a two fold meaning: (1) To show pity, compassion and active kindness toward the destitute, and (2) to soften or deter judgment on the guilt-ridden. It is likely that Jesus intended both meanings when He said, *Blessed are the merciful: for they shall obtain mercy.*

In light of this understanding, therefore, we could interpret the Beatitude to mean, "Blessed are those who show pity, compassion and active kindness toward the destitute."

No one is better able to manifest this attitude than one who has himself experienced destitution. As we saw when we studied the first Beatitude, destitution and poverty of spirit are closely related.

Early in my ministry, I understood that mercifulness and compassion were qualities greatly to be desired. I coveted them, but couldn't quite grasp how to possess them. Another minister of my acquaintance extolled their virtues and urged us to have them, but, as is all too commonly the case, he failed to prescribe how to obtain them. But with the passing of the years and the maturing of experience, I have found that experience itself is the best teacher. Experiencing destitution, in whatever form it may come, teaches compassion and mercifulness most effectively.

A Canadian gentleman related an amazing story to me that clearly illustrates this truth. He said that when his mother died, his father was so grief-smitten that he could hardly live. His pastor and friends sought in vain to comfort him. He sat in his house day after day in the agony of his sorrow, and it seemed there would be no remedy for him.

Then one day a farmer friend came to his home. He entered the room of his sorrowing friend, but did not speak a word. He simply seated himself beside the smitten man, took his hand in his own big hand, and held it for about twenty minutes. Then he left, as he had come, without uttering a word.

Amazingly the cloud of sorrow lifted and the sorrowing man found God's healing balm.

What made the difference? The visiting farmer had walked a similar road of devastating sorrow earlier, making possible the communication of his healing empathy and compassion, which, without words, reached to the spirit of his downcast friend and gave him a new lease on life.

King David affords a graphic example of mercifulness, and it is not difficult to show that his mercifulness grew out of his own desperate need for mercy.

He knew utter destitution, even in his youthful years when he was chased like a wild animal by the wicked King Saul. His refuge had been caves and forests as he fled like a bird from the snare. Distressed, distraught and deeply perplexed, he had pondered his awful plight, unable to reconcile his heart-rending experience with God's call and promises.

Yet he was not alone. His own destitution drew the destitute toward him. *And every one that was in distress, and every one that was in debt, and every one that was discontented, gathered themselves together unto him; and he became a captain over them: and there were with him about four hundred men* (Sam. 22:2).

He recognized his own overwhelming poverty. *But I am poor and needy...*(Psa. 40:17). *But I am poor and needy: make haste unto me, O God: thou art my help and my deliverer; O Lord, make no tarrying* (Psa. 70:5).

He partook of mourning and grief over his deplorable condition:

> *I am weary with my groaning; all the night make I my bed to swim; I water my couch with my tears. Mine eye is consumed because of grief; it waxeth old because of all mine enemies. Depart from me, all ye workers of iniquity; for the Lord hath heard the voice of my weeping. The Lord hath heard my supplication; the Lord will receive my prayer* (Psa. 6:6-9).

Attend unto me, and hear me: I mourn in my complaint, and make a noise (Psa. 55:2).

He was reduced to such meekness as to become a shadow of the Messiah, with whom he seemed to identify himself in the great Messianic Psalm when he exclaimed, *The meek shall eat and be satisfied* ...(Psa. 22:26).

And he hungered and thirsted after righteousness. It was his deepest craving. Hear him cry, *As the hart panteth after the water brooks, so panteth my soul after thee, O God. My soul thirsteth for God, for the living God: when shall I come and appear before God?* (Psa. 42:1-2). He longed for God-likeness. *I shall be satisfied, when I awake, with thy likeness* (Psa.17:15).

Little wonder then that he should have been such a master at showing mercy, pity, compassion and active kindness, not only toward those who were needy and worthy of it, but even toward the wicked Saul who employed every energy and means in his effort to destroy David.

Epitomizing his most exemplary mercifulness is his treatment of Mephibosheth, the son of Jonathan, and grandson of Saul. By the standards of the day he had every right to destroy Mephibosheth, for then it was common to eliminate any progeny of a deposed king.

But this was not David's response. He must show mercy. Mephibosheth's situation was the saddest of stories. When he was only five, his father and grandfather were killed in one day. His mother may have been dead, for he was cared for by a nurse. Upon hearing the evil tidings of Jonathan's and Saul's death at the hands of the Philistines, the terrified nurse sought to flee, bearing the child in her arms. But in her haste, she stumbled, falling upon the child and maiming the little prince for life.

Even so, she succeeded in preserving his life, and carried him to Lo-debar in northern Gilead where he grew to manhood and later married.

He begat a son, Micha; but his life, despite the fact that he had barely escaped an early death, was a series of disasters, disappointments and anxieties. "It was a weary, broken, dispirited soul that speaks in all his utterances." [10]

Nevertheless, when David was well-established in the kingdom, rather than seeking vengeance against his avowed enemy Saul, and his household, he literally sought opportunity for showing mercy. And David said, *Is there yet any that is left of the house of Saul, that I may show him kindness...?* (2 Sam. 9:1).

The merciful at heart do not have to look long and hard for opportunities for showing mercy, for the world around us is full of people who desperately need it.

David found it to be so as well. *And there was of the house of Saul a servant whose name was Ziba. And when they had called him unto David, the king said unto him, Art thou Ziba? And he said, Thy servant is he. And the king said, Is there not yet any of the house of Saul, that I may show the kindness of God unto him? And Ziba said unto the king, Jonathan hath yet a son, which is lame on his feet* (Sam. 9:2-3).

> *Upon discovering Mephibosheth, David lavished upon him his mercy and his kindness all the remaining days of his life. And David said unto him, Fear not: for I will surely show thee kindness for Jonathan thy father's sake, and will restore thee all the land of Saul thy father; and thou shalt eat bread at my table continually. And he bowed himself, and said, What is thy servant, that thou shouldest look upon such a dead*

> *dog as I am? Then the king called to Ziba, Saul's servant, and said unto him, I have given unto thy master's son all that pertained to Saul and to all his house....And all that dwelt in the house of Ziba were servants unto Mephibosheth. So Mephibosheth dwelt in Jerusalem: for he did eat continually at the king's table; and was lame on both his feet.*
>
> (2 Sam. 9:7-9, 12-13)

Yes, *Blessed are the merciful: for they shall obtain mercy.*

A mere three years after he had begun extending such generous and godly mercy to the household of Saul, David found himself in desperate need of similar mercy, for he had fallen into the most despicable sins of adultery, murder and deception.

Now he deserved to die. The Law proclaimed it in no uncertain terms. What hope is there for such a sinner? And David himself, upon hearing the parable of the poor man and his lamb (see 2 Sam. 12:1-4) from the mouth of God's prophet Nathan whom God had sent to awaken him to his awful guilt, pronounced his own proper and deserved judgment when he angrily declared, *As the Lord liveth, the man that hath done this thing shall surely die* (2 Sam. 12:5).

How like most humans he was. It is so easy to discern the guilt of others and to demand justice for them while all the while we are somehow blinded to our own guilt. Paul spoke of it to the Romans when he said, *Thou that sayest a man should not commit adultery, dost thou commit adultery?* (Rom. 2:22).

The Law could offer no promise of life to David. Only death. How could David escape this rightful consequence of his unlawful and ungodly deeds? There was only one way. By grace alone. Grace is the mother of all mercy. The Davidic Covenant had assured God's people of the availability of His grace. *If he commit iniquity* (indicating that God foresaw such a prospect even as He foresaw the same prospect for all humans), *I will chasten him with the rod of men, and with the stripes of the children of men: but my mercy shall not depart away from him* (2 Sam. 7:14-15).

Blessed are the merciful: for they shall obtain mercy. David had sown mercy. Therefore, he could reap mercy. Mercy may not ever be earned, but an attitude of mercifulness opens the door for God's extended mercy. *And Nathan said unto David The Lord also hath put away thy sin; thou shalt not die* (2 Sam. 12:13).

Opportunities for showing mercy abound. A hurting world cries for mercy, for pity, for compassion and for active kindness, and those who provide these qualities in their outreach to others position themselves to receive God's reciprocal mercy in their behalf.

A second interpretation of the fifth Beatitude could be aptly stated as, "Blessed are those who soften or deter judgment."

Beware of the man who cries for justice and insists on the full thirty-nine stripes for the offender. *For he shall have judgment without mercy, that hath shown no mercy; and mercy rejoiceth against judgment* (James 2:13).

The quality of mercy is not strained;
It droppeth as gentle rain from heaven
Upon the place beneath. It is twice blessed:
It blesseth him who gives, and him who takes:
'Tis mightiest in the mightiest: it becomes
The throned monarch better than his crown.
It is an attribute of God himself;
And earthly power doth then show likest God's

When mercy seasons justice —
Though justice by thy plea, consider this,
That, in the course of justice, none of us
Should see salvation. We do pray for mercy;
And that same prayer doth teach us all to render
The deeds of mercy —
Why, all the souls that are, were forfeit once:
And he who might the 'vantage best have took
Found out the remedy. How would you be,
If He who is the top of judgment should
But judge you as you are? O, think on that;
And mercy then will breathe within your lips,
Like man, new made.
How shalt thou hope for mercy, rend'ring none?[11]

I remember well my first lesson on mercy as it relates to judgment. Two of my brothers and I were close in age to one another. Being typical boys, we were quite inclined to mischief and were frequently given to misbehaving around our farm home. One day, after a siege of untoward behavior, our tiny mother threatened us with, "Boys, if you don't settle down and begin behaving, all you will get for Christmas is a big stick!" We couldn't conceive of such severity coming to us, so we continued our misbehaving about as usual.

Then came Christmas Eve with all its glorious anticipation. Our stockings were hung on the kitchen wall and excitement was high. Mother took the three of us to the attic. That, in itself, was a time-consuming feat. A stairway led to the second floor of the home, but there was no stairway to the attic. I don't remember exactly how we got up there, but finally we made it. Our purpose was to examine some cheese which had been placed there for curing.

All of this was, of course, a ploy to kill some time. The cheese was carefully unwrapped and a slice was given to each of us. Finally, after an overly long process, the cheesecloth had to be resewn and the package rewrapped. Once these tasks were completed, mother released us, and like bucking broncos released from rodeo chutes, we escaped the attic and went thundering down the stairway to the kitchen. The surprise of our lives awaited us there.

Judgment, and I might add well-deserved judgment, met us head-on. There, in every stocking, was the promised "big stick." What an awful moment.

Just when our grief and regret were at their peak, dad, with his big hand of mercy, wiped away our judgment and swung open the door to the front room where a beautiful tree laden with lights and gifts dominated our view.

Our heavenly Father is like that. He is merciful. He has a mercy seat. He is *rich in mercy* (Eph. 2:4). He is abundantly merciful (see 1 Pet. 1:3). *But the mercy of the Lord is from everlasting to everlasting...* (Psa. 103-17). Twenty-six times in a single Psalm (Psalm 136) it is stated, *his mercy endureth forever.*

How then can the believer who would conform to the image of the Son who is the "express image of his (God's) person," be less than merciful?

Put on therefore, as the elect of God, holy and beloved, bowels of mercies, kindness, humbleness of mind, meekness, longsuffering; forbearing one another, and forgiving one another, if any man have a quarrel against any: even as Christ forgave you, so also do ye (Col. 3:12-13).

But the wisdom that is from above is first pure, then peaceable, gentle, and easy to be entreated, full of mercy and good fruits, without partiality, and without hypocrisy. And the fruit of righteousness is sown in peace of them that make peace (James 3:17-18).

Blessed are the merciful: for they shall obtain mercy.

6

Seeing is Knowing

Blessed are the pure in heart: for they shall see God (Matt. 5:8).

Once man has discovered his spiritual impoverishment, mourned over his utter destitution, arrived at the gateway to meekness and entered upon its arena, been infused with a righteousness not his own, and mercifulness has displaced his attitude of unconcern and judgmentalism to his fellowman, then and only then is he truly ready for genuine confrontation with his soul's holy of holies, with its sanctuary of the sacred. This may be the soul's point of greatest pain and anguish, the place of its own Gethsemane and Golgotha.

It is also the place of its highest prospect — seeing God.

Purity of heart is the believer's pearl of great price. It is his most coveted treasure because it alone can open wide the door to the beatific vision of seeing God.

So what did our Lord have in mind when He challenged us to have a pure heart?

Purity of heart, it must be understood, is a certain state, a condition. Beyond that, it is an attitude, a mind-set, a posture of the soul, a bent of the inner man. It encompasses both positive and negative aspects.

> God did not choose some because He foresaw their holiness, but in order that they might become"holy and without blame." These two terms denote the positive and negative sides of purity: holy — possessed of the fruits of the Spirit (Gal. V. 22, 23); without blame or blemish — marked by no stain of imperfection. [12]

While purity of heart speaks to righteousness of being, it also addresses rightness of attitude toward sin and evil. *Thou hast loved righteousness, and hated iniquity; therefore God, even thy God, hath anointed thee with the oil of gladness above they fellows* (Heb. 1:9).

Purity of heart is clear, bright, transparent sincerity that is free from any hint of deception. It has no perverse motive, no selfish aims or agendas, underlying a fair exterior. Its aim is to be, not to seem to be. The pure in heart are free from corrupting thoughts, those evil and wicked imaginations, those unholy deeds designated by such terms as "unclean" and "impure," that kind of defilement which grips the imagination, stains the whole heart and mind, utterly separates the soul from seeing God, and which comes first to our attention when this Beatitude confronts us.

Thus purity of heart might be considered to be the most significant thread in the whole divine tapestry depicting *the measure of the stature of the fullness of Christ.*

Before inquiring into the means to attain to this highly-to-be-coveted-and-treasured possession, it is imperative that its qualities be understood. According to *Strong's Exhaustive Concordance,* "pure" derives from the Greek word *kathorós,* which means "clean" or "clear" while "heart" is from the Greek *kardía* meaning "the heart," i.e. the thoughts or feelings (mind)." Therefore, purity of heart has as its central focus the mind or the thoughts.

Impurity, the opposite of purity, is expressed in outward acts, and it is conceived in inward thoughts. It was to this very thing that Jesus alluded, following the Beatitudes in His Sermon on the Mount, when He said, *Ye have heard that it hath been said by them of old time, Thou shalt not commit adultery* (that is, the outward act) *but I say unto you, That whosoever looketh on a woman to lust after her* (that is, the inward thought) *hath committed adultery with her already in his heart* (Matt. 5:27-28).

Since purity of heart comprehends the whole spectrum of thoughts and motives as well as the moral dispositions and attitudes, it is among the highest aspirations of the soul. Those who strive most earnestly for it are often also those who are most plagued with the awareness of their own depravity and lack of purity. They grieve over their struggle for it, and join company with Job in crying, *Who can bring a clean thing out of an unclean? not one* (Job 14:4).

It is unthinkable that our Lord would tantalize us with an unattainable goal, like a sadist dangling a rope just beyond the reach of a drowning man. After all, it was He who said, *Blessed are the pure in heart: for they shall see God.* And David, long before our Lord's advent, announced it equally as plainly when he said, *Who shall ascend into the hill of the Lord? or who shall stand in his holy place? He that hath clean hands, and a pure heart; who hath not lifted up his soul unto vanity, nor sworn deceitfully. He shall receive the blessing from the Lord, and righteousness from the God of his salvation* (Psa. 24:3-5).

The fact is, purity of heart is attainable. It is within our reach, yet it is not obtained by the mere works or energy of man. Asceticism or the confines of the cloister cannot produce it. Mutilation of the body cannot accomplish it, though Jesus did say, *And if thy right eye offend thee, pluck it out, and cast it from thee: for it is profitable for thee that one of thy members should perish, and not that thy whole body should be cast into hell* (Matt. 5:29).

Obviously He did not intend to infer that the heart could be purified by any physical process, regardless of how severe it might be, but rather that purity of heart is of such great consequence that if a physical process could afford a solution it ought to be performed.

What then are the means to heart purity? What specific steps shall man take? How shall he obtain this most worthy goal?

As in all spiritual conquests, the beginning point is faith. Only God himself has the ability to purify the heart, but He can do it only in response to faith. All moral excellence in man is derived in this way and in no other. Peter made a strong point of this in his testimony to the Jews after his ministry to the "unclean" Gentiles of Cornelius's household: *And God, which knoweth the hearts, bare them witness, giving them the Holy Ghost, even as he did unto us; and put no difference between us and them, purifying their hearts by faith* (Acts 15: 8-9). When faith acts, purification of heart happens.

But purity of heart, while it is an instantaneous result of conversion, is also the fruit of a continuing process. At conversion the fountainhead is purified, but afterward contamination occurs which must be dealt with on an ongoing basis. We must be vigilant keepers of our hearts. *Above all else, guard your heart, for it is the wellspring of life* (Prov. 4:23, NIV).

Jesus alluded to this purifying process during the foot-washing ceremony described in John 13: *He that is washed needeth not save to wash his feet* (that is, from the contaminants from his daily walk) *but is clean every whit: and ye are clean...* (John 13:10).

I well remember that up to the point of my conversion my speaking was often punctuated with ungodly expletives. But then God purified my heart by faith. Not long after my new birth, my father's hired man and I were hauling a load of grain to town. As we drove along, a terrible vibration developed. Stopping to see what was wrong, we discovered a flat tire. Now, flat tires on an empty truck are one thing, but on a truck that is loaded with grain they are quite another!

Out of habit, upon seeing our dilemma, I cursed. But the moment I did so, my heart, now purified by faith, smote me. I felt so very unclean and impure. I repented immediately, and until this day, some sixty years later, no further curse words have ever passed my lips.

Someone has aptly stated, "This purity is a Christian grace; it comes from the abiding presence of the Holy Ghost who purifies the heart in which He deigns to dwell. That presence cleanses, refines, illuminates; it shines through the dark places of the heart; it shows the plague-spots, and through confession, contrition and repentance, it cleanses them away."

Thank God, there is a fountain opened for cleansing from sin and uncleanness. It is never closed. The sinful, the impure, the defiled come to it every day. For *If we confess our sins, he is faithful and just to forgive us our sins, and to cleanse us* (that is, purify us) *from all unrighteousness* (1 John 1:9).

Even so, there is an everlasting bent in all of us, even in us who are believers, to grow callous and cold and to allow the fountain of our hearts to be polluted by the impurities of the world. How vast is the multitude which falls short of the beatific vision because they wander aimlessly with their eyes blinded by the combined forces of Satan and sin.

It is not only the unbelieving world that is thus deprived of the blessed seeing of God. All too commonly it is also the Church, and even more particularly the individual within the Church. To the Laodicean church the Revelator wrote, *Because thou sayest, I am rich, and increased with goods, and have need of nothing; and knowest not that thou art...blind...* (Rev. 3:17).

To such people the Apostle James prescribed a cure:

> *Submit yourselves therefore to God. Resist the devil, and he will flee from you. Draw nigh to God, and he will draw nigh to you. Cleanse your hands, ye sinners; and purify your hearts, ye double minded. Be afflicted, and mourn, and weep: let your laughter be turned to mourning, and your joy to heaviness. Humble yourselves in the sight of the Lord, and he shall lift you up.*
>
> (James 4:7-10)

Yes, the pure in heart are indeed blessed, for they see God. What greater thing could one ever want? It is fascinatingly paradoxical that to see Him is to be like Him, while at the same time, to be like Him is to see Him. Jesus said, *The pure in heart shall see God,* and John wrote, *...we shall be like him; for we shall see him as he is* (1 John 3:2).

The question rises quite naturally: What does it mean to see God? Shall man with human eye gaze upon the Holy One in all of His majestic glory? Hardly, for God has declared, *There shall no man see me, and live* (Exod. 33:20).

It should be noted here that seeing God, while the ultimate glory of that blessedness is reserved for eternity, is most assuredly intended to be a part of our blessing now, only we cannot see Him in all His radiant glory: *For now we see through a glass, darkly; but then face to face: now I know in part; but then shall I know even as also I am known* (l Cor. 13:12).

Men look for Him now and defiantly deny His existence, because they do not see Him. Early Russian astronauts reportedly looked for Him in vain from their earth-orbiting spaceship. Some intellectuals may endeavor to use their brains to attempt to penetrate the veil of His invisibility with no success as well.

One thing is certain. He cannot be seen with human eyes. He is invisible to our natural vision. The Scriptures state it in the most positive language: *Now unto the King eternal, immortal, invisible, the only wise God, be honour and glory for ever and ever. Amen* (1 Tim. 1:17). And Paul explained to the Corinthians: *For the things which are seen (that is, with human eyes) are temporal; but the things which are not seen* (again, with human eyes) *are eternal* (2 Cor. 4:18).

Nonetheless, God can be seen, and when He is not seen, there is an evident reason. Jesus declared, *Blessed are the pure in heart, for they shall see God,* and His implication is clear — that those who are <u>not pure</u> in heart shall not see God. The Bible leaves no doubt when it observes: *The god of this world hath blinded the minds of them which believe not, lest the light of the glorious gospel of*

Christ, who is the image of God, should shine unto them (2 Cor. 4:4).

The problem is blindness of the heart. It is a type of blindness that is not easily diagnosed, and it is less easily admitted to. It is Satan's master stroke and strategy in his subtle effort at preventing man from beholding the great God in His glory. *Having the understanding darkened, being alienated from the life of God through the ignorance that is in them, because of the blindness of their heart* (Eph. 4:18).

But the pure in heart have anointed their eyes with eye salve, and now they see. The scales, as was the case with Saul of Tarsus, have fallen from their eyes and they gaze upon Him.

Theirs is a different kind of seeing. It is seeing with the eyes of their understanding as Paul prayed for the Ephesians, *the eyes of your understanding being enlightened* (Eph. 1:18). It is seeing as Moses saw. It is seeing as Paul saw. Noteworthy is the fact that the Greek word employed by Jesus for "see" is *optánomai,* which means to gaze with wide-open eyes, as at something remarkable. The word carries also the concept of perceiving or discerning. Thus it does no violence to say that to see is to know. This was evident in Paul's view when he prayed *the eyes of your understanding being enlightened; that ye may know* (Eph. 1:18). Hence to see God is to truly know God.

Later we shall see how this was demonstrated in both Moses and Paul, but consider first the serpent's temptation of the Edenic couple, and how it, in one fell swoop, opened their eyes to evil, while at the same time robbing them of their singularly high privilege of looking upon their God. *For God doth know that in the day ye eat thereof, then your eyes shall be opened, and ye shall be as gods, knowing good and evil...And the eyes of them both were opened, and they knew that they were naked?* (Gen. 3:5,7 emphasis mine). What a contrast. Satan opens men's eyes to behold impurity and evil. Purity of heart wrought by Christ and the Holy Spirit opens their eyes to behold their God.

Look at Moses. He perceived that if he was to successfully lead stubborn, stiff-necked, rebellious Israel into the Promised Land, he must have a glimpse of the invisible God. *Show me thy glory,* he pled (Exod. 33:18). This was equivalent to praying, "Show me thyself," for God's glory and His self are inseparable and virtually synonymous. His glory is the outshining, the effulgence of His goodness, His nature, His character and His being.

And God accommodated him. To Moses He said,

> *I will make all my goodness pass before thee, and I will proclaim the name of the Lord before thee; and will be gracious to whom I will be gracious, and will show mercy on whom I will show mercy...and it shall come to pass, while my glory passeth by, that I will put thee in a cleft of the rock, and will cover thee with my hand while I pass by.*
>
> (Exod. 33:19, 22)

Then follows this rather strange description of what Moses was to see: *And I will take away mine hand, and thou shalt see my back parts; but my face shall not be seen* (Exod. 33:23). What must God have meant? Was Moses to somehow, with human eyes, look upon the *invisible* God? We come nearest to knowing the answer by examining what followed.

The record indicates that Moses, in obeying God's instructions, ascended the mountain, and stood there upon Sinai with his head in the cloud and with his feet on the rock. *And Moses rose up early in the morning, and went up unto mount Sinai, as the Lord had commanded him...And the Lord descended in the cloud, and stood with him there* ...(Exod. 34:4-5).

What did Moses see in that holy moment? A mysterious physical form of some kind? Did he see some ghostlike being? An apparition? We hardly think so. For rather than seeing with his natural eyes, suddenly he is seeing through a new set of eyes — the enlightened eyes of the inner man. And in so seeing, he pierces the separating veil, and transcends the merely human and passes into the heavenly realm. He sees the all-excelling goodness of God, His divine nature, His pristine character, His righteous and holy being. He beholds enough of God — His "back parts" — to accommodate his earthly sojourn, but no more. For no mere mortal, though he ascend the highest mount of revelation, and though the eyes of his understanding be enlightened by the Holy Spirit, can probe the depths of the Eternal Being. *O the depths of the riches both of the wisdom and knowledge of God! How unsearchable are his judgments, and his ways past finding out!* (Rom. 11:33).

Whether Moses' physical eyes saw anything we cannot say, and it really matters not at all. What counts is that what he saw with "enlightened eyes" impacted upon his life and his mission immeasurably, and this sustained him throughout the remaining years of his leadership.

The account of what he saw is clear:

> *The Lord, the Lord God, merciful and gracious, longsuffering and abundant in goodness and truth, keeping mercy for thousands, forgiving iniquity and*

transgression and sin, and that will by no means clear the guilty; visiting the iniquity of the fathers upon the children, and upon the children's children, unto the third and to the fourth generation.

(Exod. 34:6-7)

He actually saw God in two dimensions, though the New Testament indicates or suggests at least four dimensions are involved: *That ye...may be able to comprehend with all saints what is the breadth, and the length, and depth, and height* (Eph. 3:17-18).

First Moses saw Him in His goodness dimension, and in four different aspects of it:

(1) The Mercy Aspect — "Merciful." What a coveted revelation for mortal man, living and struggling under an innate sense of guilt and impending judgment! And what would have been a greater revelation to Moses who struggled and agonized over the broken Law with its promise of certain death for the people he was leading?

The truth broke upon him like a bright light in awful darkness. He saw what all men need to see — that "mercy rejoiceth against judgment" (James 2:13), and that "His mercy endureth forever" (Psa. 136).

Our Heavenly Father is a God of great mercy. Now Moses really knew it. To see is to know.

(2) The Grace Aspect — "Gracious." Mercy and grace are closely related. Mercy is that act whereby God refrains from giving us what we deserve; grace is that act whereby he gives us what we do not deserve.

To see God is to see His grace. Moses now saw Him as the God whose grace was sufficient for his earthly pilgrimage, and the vision was likely enhanced by the dark backdrop of Israel's great need.

John saw God in the same light: *And we beheld his glory, the glory as of the only begotten of the Father full of grace* (John 1:14). Paul perceived the same truth and wrote: *For ye know the grace of our Lord Jesus Christ, that, though he was rich, yet for your sakes he became poor, that ye through his poverty might be rich* (2 Cor. 8:9).

(3) The Longsuffering Aspect — "Longsuffering." Man tends to conceive of God in his own image. He is inclined to impatience. Thus he conceives of God in the same fashion. No doubt Moses did. He feared God's patience with Israel was exhausted and that God would surely destroy His people. But now his vision was cleared and Moses saw Him as the God who is longsuffering.

What a grand revelation for guilt-ridden and sin-prone humanity. *The Lord...is longsuffering to us-ward, not willing that any should perish, but that all should come to repentance* (2 Pet. 3:9).

Add to these three aspects — mercy, grace and longsuffering — abundance in goodness and truth, and with Moses you encompass the whole beatific vision of the goodness dimension of God. But lest Moses should misjudge God and consequently mislead Israel, he had to see another dimension of the same God — the severity dimension. *And that will by no means clear the guilty; visiting the iniquity of the fathers upon the children, and upon the children's children, unto the third and to the fourth generation* (Exod. 34:7).

That terrible prospect is only for those who reject the goodness aspect of God and thus disregard the Spirit of grace.

This is an insert to correct a printing error. Sorry!

On page 71, replace paragraph 2 with these two paragraphs.

What impact did seeing God have upon Moses? He had had a pure heart. He had seen God. He had indeed been blessed. *And Moses made haste, and bowed his head toward the earth and worshipped* (Exod. 34:8). And from thence he went forth patiently preparing Israel for the Promised Land.

Few men have seen God as Paul saw Him. He saw Him first in the person of His Son on the Damascus road. His testimony was, *And last of all he was seen of me also, as of one born out of due time* (I Cor. 15:8). The affect of that singular revelation was so intense and so genuine that it blinded his physical eyes, leaving him in that state for three days, and forever altering his life-style.

Judas is an example. He willfully rejected the goodness dimension of God. He left no alternative, for God will not clear the guilty. Judas cast aside the only means of escaping his guilt. He disregarded the Spirit of grace. *There remained only a certain fearful looking for of judgment and fiery indignation, which shall devour the adversaries* (Heb. 10:27).

What impact did seeing God have upon Moses? He had had a pure heart. He had seen God. He had indeed been blessed. *And Moses made haste, and bowed his head toward the earth, and worshipped* (Exod. 34:8). The effect of that singular revelation was so intense and so genuine that it blinded his physical eyes, leaving him in that state for three days, and forever altering his life-style.

Beyond that experience, Paul saw God in such a profound way as to make him an authority on seeing God and a teacher for all who may aspire to see Him. He saw Him and he knew Him, and he was immeasurably consumed thereafter with a passion for seeing and knowing Him to an even greater degree personally, and that his fellow-Christians would join him in his quest.

Examine his prayers. In all of them his dominant concern is that God's people may see and know Him. He clearly understood that such a lofty goal could not be gained by human intellect. As one has observed, "God is an object for the heart more than for the intellect, and the eyes of our heart, more than our intellect, have been filmed over by sin."

This was a great concern to Paul, and it surfaced in his First Epistle to the Corinthians, where he wrote, "But as it is written, *Eye hath not seen, nor ear heard, neither have entered into the heart of man, the things which God hath prepared for them that love him* (1 Cor. 2:9).

Yet Paul was not content with leaving the Corinthians suspended on so negative a prognosis. His heart was intent on their seeing God, knowing God and knowing the things God had prepared for them. He had, before his conversion when blindness reigned in his heart, zealously sought to destroy the Church. He had resorted to all of the resources of his steel-like mind, and to his Sanhedrin-assigned authority, to eliminate what he perceived to be little more than a cultic threat to his beloved Judaism. But then he had met Jesus face to face, and all of that was changed. He had begun seeing beyond anything he had seen. He had begun seeing God, and knowing Him at a level unknown to him before. He began hearing from another world.

Beyond his jolting Damascus Road experience, he had most profoundly entered into his vast new understanding of these things during a possible extended stint in the Arabian desert. There he had beheld what no human eye had ever gazed upon. He had heard beyond the capability of human ears. And he had come to this knowledge in a way that defied apprehension by the human mind. Commenting on the process by which he had entered this arena, he said, *For I neither received it of man, neither was I taught it, but by the revelation of Jesus Christ* (Gal. 1:12).

We tend to shy away from anything that is labeled "revelation," and indeed we must exercise caution for many strange aberrations have borne that label. Nonetheless, the things which God has prepared for them that love Him cannot be known apart from it. Paul knew this truth with certainty. Thus he prayed with a heart that had been purified by faith and a passion for the church at Ephesus.

What then can we know about these things that seem to be so shrouded in mystery? Can we see God? Can we truly know Him? Interestingly enough, Paul makes no elaborate attempt at articulating his profound perceptions. It is likely that the reason for this is that every man who would have such revelations and perceptions must walk the same course and obtain them from the same source.

The pure in heart shall see God. These very things eluded the princes of this world, *For had they known it, they would not have crucified the Lord of glory* (1 Cor. 2:8). The natural man, be he ever so clever and academically equipped, cannot in anywise surmount the barriers to this knowledge and penetrate the veil. The unspiritual, the unholy, the defiled are out of court when it comes to judging such matters. They are like the deaf judging music or the blind appraising a Rembrandt.

Yes, there are things prepared for us which have not yet been revealed to our hearts. There are depths and heights of understanding that beg our discovery. There are things waiting to be revealed by the Spirit. There are deep things of God. There is God himself. There are things freely given to us of God. There are spiritual things. There are things which the natural man cannot receive. There is seeing God and knowing Him.

All of these things are scarcely unveiled, as if to whet our appetites as Jesus did when He said, *Blessed are the pure in heart: For they shall see God.* They are like the tell-tale surface of a beautiful Montana agate barely peeking through the earth's surface, awaiting discovery by the diligent pursuer.

We may gain a final lesson on seeing God from Job. The sequence in the process indicated in the Beatitudes is not difficult to trace in his experience. Remember his poverty of spirit, his utter destitution. *Naked came I out of my mother's womb, and naked shall I return thither: the Lord gave, and the Lord hath taken away; blessed be the name of the Lord* (Job 1:21)

Remember his mourning over his condition. *Oh that my grief were thoroughly weighed, and my calamity laid in the balances together! For now it would be heavier than the sand of the sea: therefore my words are swallowed up* (Job 6:2-3).

Recall his meekness, *Though he slay me, yet will I trust in him: but I will maintain mine own ways before him. He also shall be my salvation* (Job 13:15-16).

His hunger and thirst after righteousness are easily discovered. *Behold, I go forward, but he is not there; and backward, but I cannot perceive him: on the left hand, where he doth work, but I cannot behold him: he hideth himself on the right hand, that I cannot see him: but he knoweth the way that I take: when he hath tried me, I shall come forth as gold* (Job 23:8-10).

And his mercifulness is self-evident. *And the Lord turned the captivity of Job, when he prayed for his friends* (Job 42:10).

Job had experienced destitution. He had mourned. He had come to meekness. He had hungered and thirsted for righteousness. He had espoused an attitude of mercifulness. His heart had been purified, and now he was ready for the blessing: *I have heard of thee by the hearing of the ear: but now mine eye seeth thee* (Job 42:5). He saw God!

Blessed are the pure in heart: for they shall see God.

7

Peacemakers

Blessed are the peacemakers: for they shall be called the children of God (Matt. 5:9).

No peacemaker will ever compare to the son of God, for He is the Prince of Peace; yet Jesus said, *How blest are the peacemakers; God shall call them his sons* (Matt. 5:9 NEB)

Peacemakers — sons. What lofty aspirations! What a beautiful thread in the divine tapestry.

But where do peacemakers come from? How are they generated? What are their components? How can anyone become a peacemaker, and thus be blessed?

Peacemakers are made. They are not the products of chance or accident. They are really composites of all of the attitudes of the Beatitudes. They are all of those attitudes wrapped in a single bundle. The genuine peacemaker has first discovered his own poverty of spirit. He has mourned over it until he has come to personal peace. He has espoused meekness, and he has hungered and thirsted for righteousness until he has been filled. Out of this has flowed both an attitude of mercifulness, so necessary to the peacemaking, and purity of heart, so vital a characteristic for the reconciler.

Peace is a fruit of righteousness. *And the work of righteousness shall be peace; and the effect of righteousness quietness and assurance forever* (Isa. 32:17). The key component in peace is righteousness. Therefore, righteousness is a fundamental prerequisite for the peacemaker. Christ Jesus our Lord is first our righteousness, then He is our peace.

Peacemaking relates to four areas in particular: (1) To man's relation with God; (2) To Jewish relations with Gentiles; (3) To man's relations with man; and finally (4) To the relation of unbelievers with God. Each of these will be considered as we move along.

1. Man's Relation With God. From a biblical perspective all men were enemies of God. *For if, when we were enemies, we were reconciled to God by the death of his Son...* (Rom. 5:10). *And you, that were sometime alienated and enemies in your mind by wicked works...* (Col. 1:21). *...know ye not that the friendship of the world* (that is, the present world system encompassing all ungodliness) *is enmity with God?* (James 4:4).

The answer to enmity is reconciliation. But reconciliation calls for a peacemaker. Yet in order for a peacemaker to make peace between enemies, he must find a means of dealing with the offense which produced his enmity. Man's unrighteousness, which produced his enmity against God, had to be dealt with before reconciliation was possible, for *There is no peace, saith my God, to the wicked* (Isa. 57:21).

Only righteous men have peace with God. Therefore, the Peacemaker had to find a means for removing the offense and thus justifying the unrighteous so that the enmity could be dispelled, and once again man could be the friend of God.

This is what the work of the great Peacemaker is all about. This is what Gethsemane is all about. This is what Golgotha is all about. This is what the cross is all about. This is what the Resurrection is all about. All of these were incorporated into the Peacemaker's effort at dealing with the offense which had broken the relation of the creature with his Creator.

Gethsemane, it can be said, was the Peacemaker's first mighty step following His incarnation toward reconciling sinful man with the holy God. It was, in some respects, the most difficult. It required an hour so desperate that in His flesh, He would like to have avoided it. *Now is my soul troubled; and what shall I say? Father, save me from this hour: but for this cause came I unto this hour* (John 12:27). The cause was peace between the offended and the offender.

Gethsemane is the place where man's offenses were dealt with in a singular way. It is the place where the long shadow of Leviticus 16:21 became substance! *And Aaron shall lay both his hands upon the head of the live goat, and confess over him all the iniquities of the children of Israel, and all their transgressions in all their sins, putting them upon the head of the goat....*

It is the place where the Peacemaker became the scapegoat, where the heavenly Father (typified by the high priest) transferred all of the offenses of all of the offenders among men to His own Son. That alone accounts for His incredible agony in the Garden, and for His desperate plea that He might avoid the dreaded "cup." It alone explains the "megaload" that pressed the blood from His veins, and caused His sweat to become as great drops of blood falling to the ground.

It was not the mere dread of death on a cross, though we would in no way diminish that, but if that had been the case, many of His followers were braver than He. Nay, rather, it was that in Gethsemane He was asked by the Father to become everything in every offender that God must judge. There it was, as Paul indicated, that, *He hath made him to be sin for us, who knew no sin; that we might be made the righteousness of God in him* (2 Cor. 5:21).

But Gethsemane was not enough. Gethsemane apart from Golgotha was an exercise in futility, even as Golgotha apart from Gethsemane was also an exercise in futility. Both steps were necessary to the peacemaking process. In Gethsemane the Peacemaker became the sin-bearer (the offense-bearer); on Golgotha He became the sin-offering (the Atoner for the sins which He bore).

Golgotha is the place where the Peacemaker, the scapegoat, was treated as an offender in the same way the goat of Leviticus 16:21-22 was treated as an offender. Surely the goat could not himself have been an offender any more than God's Son could have been an offender, yet both were considered and treated as offenders. How great the love and grace of God! *...And shall send him away by the hand of a fit man into the wilderness: and the goat shall bear on him all their iniquities unto a land not inhabited: and shall let go the goat in the wilderness* (Lev. 16:21-22).

Such treatment for the goat let go outside the camp spelled certain death for the animal. *Wherefore Jesus also, that he might sanctify the people with his own blood, suffered without the gate* (Heb. 13:12). That was Golgotha! That was Calvary! That was the cross. There He was counted among the offenders that He might pay the ultimate penalty — death for all, and make it possible for every offender to be reconciled and at peace with the offended. *And...made peace through the blood of his cross, by him (Jesus) to reconcile all things unto himself* (God)... (Col. 1:20).

Christ's resurrection was a vital and necessary step in the peace process. It was the capstone. It was the guarantee that the offenses had been properly disposed of, and that man could now stand before God, not any longer as an enemy, but as His friend. *Who was delivered for our offences, and was raised again for our justification* (Rom. 4:25).

> *But not as the offence, so also is the free gift. For if through the offence of one many be dead, much more the grace of God, and the gift by grace, which is by one man, Jesus Christ, hath abounded unto many. And not as it was by one that sinned, so is the gift: for the judgement was by one to condemnation, but the free gift is of many offences unto justification. For if by one man's offence death reigned by one; much more they which receive abundance of grace and of the gift of righteousness shall reign in life by one, Jesus Christ. Therefore as by the offence of one judgment came upon all men to condemnation; even so by the righteousness of one the free gift came upon all men unto justification of life. For as by one man's disobedience many were made sinners, so by the obedience of one shall many be made righteous.*
>
> (Rom. 5:15-19)

The Peacemaker, the Prince of Peace, had made it possible for enemies to become friends, not by overlooking the offenses which had caused the separation, but by satisfying the penalty imposed by the offenses. Blessed is the Peacemaker, for He is the Son of God!

Yet, even though peace is provided by the Peacemaker, it must be appropriated by the offender. When this is done, the offender in turn becomes a peacemaker, that is, he himself makes peace with God, and when he does, he experiences the blessedness of the Beatitude, *Blessed are the peacemakers: for they shall be called the children of God.*

2. Jewish Relations With Gentiles. Man's enmity against God found its manifestation in enmity between Jew and Gentile, between what was perceived to be holy and that which was unholy, between the children of God and the heathen, between the circumcision and the uncircumcision. The Jews thought of the Gentiles as "dogs," and proudly considered themselves to be a superior race while the Gentiles regarded the Jews as exclusionists and enemies of humanity.

Even in the Jewish Temple enmity between Jew and Gentile seems to have been evident, for there was a boundary separating the two, beyond which the Gentiles were forbidden to pass.

The enmity between Jews and Gentiles, though it may be traced to Abraham's time (when circumcision was first introduced, for that began the quarrel), is also attributable, at least in part, to Israel's own rebellion and disobedience toward God. When that happened, not only did Israel become God's enemy, but every man became Israel's enemy.

Deuteronomy prophetically paints the picture very graphically:

> *And it shall come to pass, that as the Lord rejoiced over you to do you good, and to multiply you; so the Lord will rejoice over you to destroy you, and to bring you to nought; and ye shall be plucked from off the land whither thou goest to possess it. And the Lord shall*

scatter thee among all people, from the one end of the earth even unto the other; and there thou shalt serve other gods, which neither thou nor thy fathers have known, even wood and stone. And among these nations shalt thou find no ease, neither shall the sole of thy foot have rest: but the Lord shall give thee there a trembling heart, and failing of eyes, and sorrow of mind: and thy life shall hang in doubt before thee; and thou shalt fear day and night, and shalt have none assurance of thy life: in the morning thou shalt say, Would God it were even! and at even thou shalt say, Would God it were morning! for the fear of thine heart wherewith thou shalt fear, and for the sight of thine eyes which thou shalt see. And the Lord shall bring thee into Egypt again with ships, by the way whereof I spake unto thee, Thou shalt see it no more again: and there ye shall be sold unto your enemies for bondmen and bondwomen, and no man shall buy you.

(Deut. 28:63-68)

That enmity continues. No people under the sun has found itself among so many enemies in every land and on every continent. Anti-semitism raises its ugly head wherever Jews are found. Peace with other nations and peoples frequently seems to elude them, and enmity from many nations is their common lot.

What is the solution to this distressing and disconcerting problem? Valiant efforts of men fail to avail much change in these deeply entrenched attitudes. Secretary James Baker and other U. S. Secretaries of State have nobly expended their energies in a "mega-effort" toward peace, mainly between Israel and her neighbors. Yet it is certain Israel as a nation will know no genuine, lasting peace apart from the Prince of Peace himself. The day for that peace is coming!

Nevertheless, in this very hour both Jew and Gentile can have peace, both with God and between each other. While the enmity existed for a millennium and a half before Jesus came, it found its solution for all who will avail themselves of it in Christ's death on the cross.

> *For he is our peace, who hath made both one, and hath broken down the middle wall of partition between us; having abolished in his flesh the enmity, even the law of commandments contained in ordinances; for to make in himself of twain one new man, so making peace; and that he might reconcile both unto God in one body by the cross, having slain the enmity thereby: and came and preached peace to you which were afar off, and to them that were nigh. For through him we both have access by one Spirit unto the Father.*
>
> (Eph. 2:14-18)

The author of peace is the Christ. The means of peace is the cross. "The world has made many efforts to unite men on a basis of liberty, equality, and fraternity — often trying to bring about a union even by the most terrible bloodshed; but no principle has yet been discovered to unite man to man save the gospel of Christ, with its doctrine of atonement through the blood of the cross." [13]

The work of Christ, we might say His peace effort, was, first of all, to provide peace with God for both Jews and Gentiles, and then to bring them to peace with each other. Man's enmity with his fellowman is usually the fruit of his enmity against God. Thus when the issue is settled with God, the foundation is laid for peace with men.

Blessed is the Peacemaker: for He is the Son of God! *Blessed are the peacemakers: for they shall be called the children of God.*

The Peacemaker's cross broke down the walls — the wall which separated man from God, and the "middle wall of partition between us," that is the wall separating Jew and Gentile, and the wall separating both from God.

Now both Jew and Gentile, born again of the Spirit, are one. There is no difference, *There is neither Jew nor Greek* (Gentile), *there is neither bond nor free, there is neither male nor female; for ye are all one in Christ Jesus* (Gal. 3:28). Both constitute one body, both grow into an holy temple unto the Lord, both make up the city of God, the Church, and the Bride for the Lamb. Both are at peace with God and with each other.

3. Man's Relation With God. Peacemaking, as we have seen, has to do with man coming to peace with God. It has to do with Jews and Gentiles coming to peace with each other and with God. But equally important is man's coming to peace with his fellowman in a more general sense, and particularly within the Christian community.

While peace with our fellowman has very broad implications, reaching as far as to relations between governments and kingdoms of this world, our consideration will center on lower levels of structure within human society — peace between individual Christians, between church members, peace within Christian families, within church organizations, within the Christian community and within the workaday world.

Who has not witnessed enmity, conflict, warring, quarreling and factions within the Christian arena? These things have plagued the Church from its earliest beginnings, and they are the devil's delight. The Apostle James, in his epistle, written only some thirty years after Christ's death, addressed the problem: *What causes wars, and what causes fighting among you? Is it not your passions that are at war in your members? You desire and do not have; so you kill. And you covet and cannot obtain; so you fight and wage war* (James 4:1-2 RSV).

Clearly, the field is wide open for peacemakers. Need and opportunity exist on every hand. The door is ajar for anyone who would covet the blessing of being called a child of God by being a peacemaker.

Heading the list of qualities and qualifications for the peacemaker, in the Christian context, is the need for having personally partaken of the divine nature: *Whereby are given unto us exceeding great and precious promises: that by these ye might be partakers of the divine nature...* (2 Pet. 1:4).

Peace is an integral part of the divine nature. *For God is...the author of...peace* (1 Cor. 14:33). Jesus said, *...My peace I give unto you* (John 14:27). Thus it can be said that He is the author and essence of peace.

Therefore, to possess that divine nature is to have taken step one toward becoming a peacemaker.

A working knowledge of the Word of God and an ear tuned to the Holy Spirit are also of inestimable value to the peacemaker. By the Word of God the principles of peace are learned; and by the Spirit of God, gifts, such as the word of wisdom, the word of knowledge and discerning of spirits can enable the peacemaker to function most effectively.

Peacemaking is a deliberate act. Some are by nature inclined toward peacemaking, but all who would be effective in the field need certain qualifications. It takes little effort to be a trouble-maker, but it takes great character to be a peacemaker.

> The Christian is not to shut himself in monastic seclusion, indifferent to the evils of the world around him. He is to interfere for its betterment. Peace is the greatest interest of nations, brotherhood the greatest requisite of society. Happy are they who can bring about such things. The process is dangerous and likely to be misunderstood, for the peacemaker is often regarded as an enemy by both sides of the quarrel. His reward, however, is great — to be accounted one of God's sons, like the only begotten Son, who is the Prince of Peacemakers. [14]

Attitude is extremely important. A peaceful, compassionate, concerned attitude will generate an atmosphere that becomes very helpful in quieting the storm. A belligerent attitude, on the other hand, on the part of a would-be peacemaker, will likely add fuel to the fire. It is the *peaceful who* become *peacemakers.*

Fairness and impartiality are indispensable. The peacemaker cannot take sides.

A fellow-minister once asked me, while I was serving as the District Superintendent for my denomination, that should I be called upon to arbitrate a dispute between a pastor and his board member, to tell him whose side I would be on. My answer was, "I would not be on either side. I would earnestly seek to discover the truth, and would attempt to be on the side of truth wherever I found it." To take sides, based upon friendship or position or any other consideration, is to disqualify one's self as a peacemaker.

On one occasion, I was invited to arbitrate a serious conflict in one of our districts. The problem had its beginnings in a local church, but it had broadened until, like leaven in a batch of dough, it had infected the entire district. Sides were formed. Lawsuits were threatened. Trouble had raised its ugly head on every hand.

I had no sooner agreed to be an arbitrator when my telephone began ringing. People used every means available to them in their effort to obtain my support for their "side." Soon I concluded the problem was too large for a single peacemaker. I needed help. And in due time arrangements were made for someone to assist me.

We were to meet at the church where the storm had begun. When the time arrived, pastor, board members, church members, district officials and interested friends gathered. The atmosphere was tense. All were wondering whose "side" the arbitrators would take.

I remember well how the concerns were quieted when I read the account of Joshua and his meeting with "the captain of the Lord's hosts." Joshua had inquired of him, *Art thou for us, or for our adversaries?* (Josh. 5:13). His answer came in a single word, "Nay," the idea being, "It is not a matter of whose side I am on; it is rather, who is on the Lord's side?" Assuring the group that we did not intend to take sides, except the Lord's side, the stage was set for the arbitration and the outcome was wonderful peace which reached to every corner of that district and continues to this day.

Integrity is mandatory. Absolute honesty is a must. The peacemaker dare not be influenced by financial considerations. He must not allow himself to be bought off. Neither must he allow political expediency to color his judgment.

Sound Judgement is his stock in trade. The peacemaker knows that in his effort at resolving enmity and trouble there is usually fault on both sides of an issue. He must be able to weigh all the evidence, and assign responsibility for the solution in an equitable manner.

Courage is another vital quality. The peacemaker must be willing to confront the issues squarely, but in an attitude of true humility. While he must avoid carelessness in disposing of them, he cannot expect to gain a lasting peace by simply glossing over the issues. As one has well said, "The peacemaker's work is not the slight healing over of a wound." The issues need to be confronted and disposed of, all the while seeking to avoid too much emotional involvement.

Qualities and qualifications are extremely important for the peacemaker, but there are noteworthy differences between peacemakers and peacemaking. Peacemaking is the process in which the peacemaker applies his peacemaking attributes.

The Scriptures exhort, *Be at peace among yourselves* (1 Thess. 5:13); *Follow peace with all men* (Heb. 12:14); *Let us therefore follow after the things which make for peace* (Rom. 14:19). We are under orders.

Peacemaking requires application and effort. It may require communication, confrontation, confession and contrition.

Peace between individual Christians is of great consequence to the ongoing ministry of the Church, for unless Christians are at peace with each other, how can they expect to attract others to the Prince of Peace? But who shall take the initiative when enmity arises between Christians? The human inclination is to insist that the other person act first. "When he comes to me, than I will forgive," we say. But it is the peacemaker who acts, and it is he who is most blessed. It is the clear teaching of the Scriptures that the initiative is *always mine,* not the other fellow's. *Moreover if thy brother shall trespass against thee, go and tell him his fault between thee and him alone* (Matt. 18:15).

Therefore if thou bring thy gift to the altar, and there rememberest that thy brother hath aught against thee; leave there thy gift before the altar, and go thy way; first be reconciled to thy brother, and then come and offer thy gift (Matt. 5:23-24).

In one church where I pastored, an incident occurred while preparations were underway for a Christmas program. As parts and recitations were assigned to the children and young people, the daughter of one board member was inadvertently overlooked. Her mother approached my wife in a rage, for my wife was the one who had given out the assignments. "Why was my daughter left out?" she questioned as she stormed out of the church in a huff.

The oversight was purely accidental, but my wife was greatly troubled by the woman's reaction. The next morning she made her way to the board member's home, and humbly acknowledging full responsibility, tearfully asked for her forgiveness. The matter was settled then and there, and the members of that family became some of our most faithful supporters.

Blessed are the peacemakers: for they shall be called the children of God.

4. The Relation of Unbelievers with God. Here is where the peacemaker can have a field day, for what can be more challenging and rewarding than making the enemies of God His friends? The truth is, every Christian is called to be a peacemaker. His is a peace mission. He is to be a member of God's "Peace Corps." He is to be chief negotiator between sinful man and the holy God.

> *Therefore if any man be in Christ, he is a new creature: old things are passed away; behold, all things*

> *are become new. And all things are of God, who hath reconciled us to himself by Jesus Christ, and hath given to us the ministry of reconciliation; to wit, that God was in Christ, reconciling the world unto himself, not imputing their trespasses unto them; and hath committed unto us the word of reconciliation. Now then we are ambassadors for Christ, as though God did beseech you by us: we pray you in Christ's stead, be ye reconciled to God.*
>
> (2 Cor. 5:17-20)

Every believer is to be an ambassador of peace. It is not his assignment to negotiate a peace between the sinner and his offended Creator. His task is to announce peace, for the peace has already been obtained. His it is to join the Great Peacemaker in declaring the ready availability of peace, and in urging men everywhere to be reconciled with God. This is possible because Jesus *came and preached peace to you which were afar off, and to them that were nigh* (Eph. 2:17).

Blessed are the peacemakers: for they shall be called the children of God.

The rewards for the peacemaker are singularly unique. The blessing of this seventh Beatitude, unlike that promised in all the Beatitudes previously considered, is not for some personal quality, attitude, virtue or grace, but for the most noble work in behalf of others, whether they be Christians, the Church or even of the world.

They shall be called the children of God or, as the Revised Standard Version puts it, *They shall be called sons of God.* We ought to remember that when the Great Peacemaker arrived on the scene of His baptism, those present for that memorable event heard a glorious announcement. *A voice from heaven, saying, This is my beloved Son, in whom*

I am well pleased (Matt. 3:17). While no other man can have that exact designation, for He was singularly the only begotten of the Father, every man who accepts His peace provision is thereafter blessed with the designation of "child of God" or "son of God." *And (I) will be a Father unto you, and ye shall be my sons and daughters, saith the Lord Almighty* (2 Cor. 6:18).

Therefore, peacemakers are, first of all, happy and blessed in themselves. They are at peace with God. They are His children, His sons.

Nevertheless, the promised blessing of being labeled child of God or a son of God has an even broader fulfillment. We can judge for ourselves. Who are the happiest people? Who do others — if not by their outward expressions, at least by their attitudes — recognize as the children of God? Does this recognition go to those who love stirring up strife, those who are easily offended, the irritable, the conceited, the cross-grained? Or does it go to those who are peacelovers, who strive for peace between themselves and others within the family, in the Church, and among friends and neighbors?

Jesus gives us the answers: *Blessed are the peacemakers: for they shall be called the children of God,* first by God himself, and then by those who are blessed with peace through the efforts of the peacemakers.

8

The Blessed Persecuted

Blessed are they which are persecuted for righteousness' sake: for theirs is the kingdom of heaven. Blessed are ye, when men shall revile you, and persecute you, and shall say all manner of evil against you falsely, for my sake. Rejoice, and be exceeding glad: for great is your reward in heaven: for so persecuted they the prophets which were before you (Matt. 5:10-12).

It sounds like a contradiction — the blessed persecuted. How can we reconcile the idea of one being persecuted and blessed at the same time? How can one who is suffering persecution be blessed of God? How can he be filled with life, joy and satisfaction? How can he be called enviably fortunate and well-off? How can he be reckoned spiritually prosperous?

Before us is the chief paradox, and it is peculiar to Christianity alone. Persecution and God's blessings do go hand in hand.

In the seven Beatitudes already considered, we have seen how the blessings of God are gained principally by attitudes and conditions that are cultivated and prevail within the human heart; but in this eighth Beatitude, God's blessings are promised to those who, because right attitudes and conditions prevail in their lives, become the targets of those who are the enemies of all righteousness. The blessings in this case are not the fruit of inward attitudes, but rather of forces arrayed against righteousness.

For some it is unthinkable that a child of God might suffer persecution. They have espoused the idea that for the child of God who has "real faith," there is no suffering, no sorrow, no affliction and certainly no persecution. For him there should be nothing but success, prosperity and happiness. His is to be a "be-happy" life-style and experience.

This approach overlooks the plain teaching of the Scriptures, *Yea, and all that will live godly in Christ Jesus shall suffer persecution* (2 Tim. 3:12). Righteousness engenders persecution like a low-pressure weather system engenders a storm.

Here in Montana, when the weatherman announces a high-pressure system over the state, we can expect no storm, no rain, nothing but Big Blue Sky. The same is true spiritually. When the "high-pressure" system of self-seeking, self-exaltation and image-improvement dominates the atmosphere, there is no spiritual rain, no revival, no seeing God and no storm of persecution.

Only when the "low-pressure" system of poverty of spirit, of mourning, of meekness, of hunger and thirst after righteousness, of mercifulness, of purity of heart, of peacefulness and peacemaking prevails, do the storm clouds of persecution begin to appear on the horizon.

Persecution ought not to be considered a strange intruder. To the contrary, its absence ought to sound an alarm, for when persecution is lacking, the Church generally tends toward dormancy and fruitlessness. Persecution kindles the fires of evangelism and assures God's blessings upon its victims.

Persecution is the hallmark of the righteous. *Now we, brethren, as Isaac was, are the children of promise. But as then he that was born after the flesh persecuted him that was born after the Spirit, even so it is now* (Gal. 4:28-29).

Forms of persecution may vary, but as certainly as there are godly men and women, so certainly will there be persecutions. As it has always been so it will always be. "Even so it is <u>now</u>." It began with ungodly Cain's persecution of his godly brother, Abel, which culminated in murder. It raised its ugly head again between the two sons of Abraham — Isaac and Ishmael.

Isaac was the fruit of faith. Ishmael was the fruit of the flesh. The persecution commenced when Isaac was a mere stripling. *And Sarah saw the son of Hagar the Egyptian, which she had born to Abraham, mocking* (Gen. 21:9). Mockery is a vicious form of persecution. It can be worse than death, for it lingers long. The word means "to laugh outright (in merriment or scorn)," and it implies "to make sport of," as when the Philistines made sport of Samson.

What child of God has not confronted "Ishmael"? He is a wild man. He is a God-mocker. He hasn't seen God. He cannot see God. He has no spiritual perception. He derides the idea of being born again. To him the experience of Pentecost is a big joke, and speaking in unknown tongues is only a psychological phenomenon. The Virgin Birth is a myth, invented to cover up immorality; and the resurrection is an hallucination, or a hoax foisted upon the public by over-zealous disciples.

Yes, let the righteous rise up, and the old dragon will stand ready to devour.

> *And there appeared a great wonder in heaven; a woman clothed with the sun, and the moon under her feet, and upon her head a crown of twelve stars: and she being with child cried, travailing in birth, and pained to be delivered. And there appeared another wonder in heaven; and behold a great red dragon, having seven heads and ten horns, and seven crowns upon his heads. And his tail drew the third part of the stars of heaven, and did cast them to the earth: and the dragon stood before the woman which was ready to be delivered, for to devour her child as soon as it was born.*
>
> (Rev. 12:1-4)

The serpent's seed is forever against the holy seed. So the child of God ought not to think *...it strange concerning the fiery trial which is to try you, as though some strange thing happened unto you* (1 Pet. 4:12). Matthew Henry says, "You must reckon upon hardships and troubles more than other men." And then he lists the forms of persecution which Christians have confronted, and may yet confront when they walk in righteousness and true holiness: "They are persecuted, hunted, pursued, run down, as noxious beasts are, they are sought for to be destroyed; as if a Christian did...bear a wolf's head, as an outlaw is said to do — any one that finds him may slay him; they are abandoned as the offscouring of all things, fined, imprisoned, banished, stripped of their estates, excluded from all places of profit and trust, scourged, racked, tortured, always delivered to death, and accounted as sheep for the slaughter." [15]

Nevertheless, these are the blessed. *Blessed are they...for theirs is the kingdom of heaven.* They do not necessarily obtain the Kingdom because they are persecuted for righteousness' sake, but they are thus persecuted because they are citizens of that Kingdom. All of what has been said to this point seems rather impersonal. It is a sort of generalization — "Blessed are *they* ...for *theirs* is the Kingdom of heaven." As a result, I think we are inclined to relate it to someone other than ourselves. Our thinking may take the following form, "Yes, others will be persecuted, and others will be blessed because of it, but not me." We tend to divorce ourselves from that scene in the same way that Jesus' disciples were inclined to do.

Therefore, Jesus turned from generalization to personalization, from "Blessed are they," to "Blessed are ye." It might be thought that Jesus was adding a ninth Beatitude, but it seems more likely that He was only enlarging on the previous concept and applying it directly to His audience, some of whom were familiar with the very evil treatment He was addressing.

"Blessed are ye *when*" ...whenever persecution visits you for the right reasons, you are already blessed. The persecution only announces the ownership of those attitudes which have provoked it.

"When men shall revile you...." That is, when men shall defame you, when they rail at you, when they chide you and taunt you, when they assign madness to you, when they label you as a neurotic, when they dub you a "holy-roller," when they regard you as sub-normal — then "rejoice and be exceeding glad."

"When men shall...persecute you." Persecution involves the idea of pursuit, with intent to harm. Persecution of the righteous is no incidental or accidental happening. It is intentional and deliberate. Even as heat applied to a pot of water causes it to boil, so the rebuke precipitated by the believer's godliness causes the ungodly to react with severity. Persecution is the normal reaction of the ungodly against the righteous. They "kick against the pricks," even as Saul of Tarsus did. His own testimony is: *And I punished them oft in every synagogue, and compelled them to blaspheme; and being exceedingly mad against them, I persecuted them even unto strange cities* (Acts 26:11).

Persecution is no respecter of persons. Wherever the godly and the ungodly are side by side it happens.

> The offense of the cross has not ceased; there is still persecution. It exists still in many households, schools, villages. The cold looks, the misrepresentations, the nicknames, the taunts, sometimes the ill-treatment of relations, fellow-servants, schoolfellows, fellow-workmen, are hard to bear.... And these modern forms of persecution are greater in extent, for they sometimes spread over a long period, and affect all the circumstances of life, and perhaps in some cases cause no less suffering than the more acute outbreaks in the old days of cruelty. [16]

We should not be surprised when it happens. Jesus said it would.

> *And Jesus answered and said, Verily I say unto you, There is no man that hath left house, or brethren, or sisters, or father, or mother, or wife, or children, or lands, for my sake, and the gospel's, but he shall receive an hundredfold now in this time, houses, and brethren, and sisters, and mothers, and children, and lands, with persecutions; and in the world to come eternal life.*
>
> (Mark 10:29-30)

When men shall...say all manner of evil against you falsely, for my sake. "Falsely" — underscore this adverb — place it in bold letters, encircle it! Woe unto us when the ungodly speak evil of us truly. Woe unto us when we, by evil deeds and unbecoming behavior give *great occasion to the enemies of the Lord to blaspheme* (2 Sam. 12:14).

The modern media and the multitudes grasp at every opportunity for speaking evil of evangelical Christianity. The ungodly have 20/20 vision for inconsistencies of Christians, and delight in exposing them mercilessly.

It is not to our credit when our behavior patterns place ammunition in their hands. When it happens, it is to our shame, and it certainly is no grounds for rejoicing and being exceedingly glad. It ought to grieve us to the core, and cause us to cry out, "Lord, deliver us from the folly of our own ways."

But when men denounce and deride us falsely for Jesus' sake, we have grounds for gladness and rejoicing. *Thou hast loved righteousness, and hated iniquity; therefore God, even thy God, hath annointed thee with the oil of gladness above thy fellows* (Heb. 1:9). The more like Jesus we are, the more likely the ungodly will be to speak evil of us. *It is enough for the disciple that he be as his master, and the servant as his lord. If they have called the master of the house Beelzebub, how much more shall they call them of his household?* (Matt. 10:25). Of Jesus they said, *Thou hast a devil* (John 7:20) and *This man blasphemeth* (Matt. 9:3). They credited His work to Satan, *But when the Pharisees heard it, they said, This fellow doth not cast out devils, but by Beelzebub the prince of devils* (Matt. 12:24).

Some of us moderns have confronted similar charges. We have been told we are of the devil. We have been labeled as evil men. All manner of evil has been spoken against us.

While in Paraguay some years ago we witnessed the phenomenal growth of our Assemblies of God churches. New churches were springing up everywhere, invading the ranks of Roman Catholicism, and many were turning to the Lord. As could have been predicted, men began to speak evil against the Pentecostals falsely for Jesus' sake. An article appeared in the newspaper in *Asuncion,* the country's largest city, ridiculing the Pentecostals and charging them with being financed by the international banking system, which was a fabricated falsehood.

My father-in-law, Bruce S. Williams, was a godly man. He served as pastor for a denominational church in the small community of Egeland, North Dakota.

During those days, his wife (my mother-in-law) experienced a remarkable infilling with the Holy Spirit, and often associated with other Pentecostals, sometimes providing housing and meals for missionaries and evangelists related to that group.

This raised the ire of some who considered Pentecostalism a cult, and although Dad Williams was not at the time a Pentecostal in experience, he and his family suffered castigation, false accusation and ill-treatment at the hands of his superiors. On one Sunday morning, for example, as he went to conduct the service he was confronted with a padlocked church door!

He was never given a proper hearing. He was simply shut out. But despite the ill-treatment, he was blessed indeed. His whole family grew up to call him blessed. All seven of his children later entered some facet of the ministry, some as pastors, some as missionaries, some as college professors and some as pastor's wives. He was persecuted, but he was blessed.

We must remember to "rejoice and be exceeding glad" for two reasons: (1) for the reward that is yet ahead, and (2) for the elite company of which you are a part.

It is quite natural and not uncommon to relate rejoicing and gladness to only pleasant circumstances and bountiful provisions, but it is certainly not natural to rejoice and be glad when evil is directed our way.

Howbeit, such thinking emanates from a wrong and perverted and worldly perspective. An attitude of true rejoicing and genuine gladness rises out of a right perspective — that reviling and persecution and false accusation are really the tell-tale indicators of Christ's righteousness reflected in us.

Who can doubt that the apostles had the right perspective? *...And...when they had called the apostles, and beaten them, they commanded that they should not speak in the name of Jesus, and let them go. And they departed from the presence of the council, rejoicing that they were counted worthy to suffer shame for his name* (Acts 5:40-41).

What are the rewards? What are the dividends afforded the suffering saints? They are both present and future; they are blessings and provisions for the perilous journey, and they are *a far more exceeding and eternal weight of glory* (2 Cor. 4:17) in heaven.

For those who are persecuted for righteousness sake, their's is the Kingdom now — righteousness and peace and joy in the Holy Ghost (see Rom 14:17); and for those who are reviled, and persecuted, and spoken against falsely for Jesus' sake, their's is great reward in heaven. For *If we suffer, we shall also reign with him* (2 Tim. 2:12).

The Beatitudes begin with the Kingdom — *Blessed are the poor in spirit: for their's is the kingdom of heaven;* and they conclude with the kingdom — *Blessed are they which are persecuted for righteousness' sake: for their's is the kingdom of heaven.*

Oh, the blessedness of those whose attitudes reflect the image of Christ!

9

The Most Blessed One

Our tapestry is now complete. The picture is finished. And what do we behold but the Son of God himself wrapped in a garment of holy attitudes? He is the epitome of all of the attitudes of the Beatitudes. His image is the ultimate. He is the blueprint for all — *Till we all come in the unity of the faith, and of the knowledge of the Son of God, unto a perfect man, unto the measure of the stature of the fulness of Christ* (Eph. 4:13).

Who better than Jesus reflects an attitude of poverty of spirit? Who can match the attitude, the mind of Christ, *Who, being in the form of God, thought it not robbery to be equal with God: but made himself of no reputation, and took upon him the form of a servant, and was made in the likeness of men: and being found in fashion as a man,...humbled himself, and became obedient unto death, even the death of the cross* (Phil. 2:6-8)?

Jesus, as in all things, shows us the way, ...*That, though he was rich, yet for your sakes he became poor, that ye through his poverty might be rich* (2 Cor. 8:9).

Jesus has manifested an attitude of mourning, not over His own poverty of spirit, but over the poverty of spirit so evident and pronounced in the human family. *O Jerusalem, Jerusalem, thou that killest the prophets, and stonest them which are sent unto thee, how often would I have gathered thy children together, even as a hen gathereth her chickens under her wings, and ye would not* (Matt. 23:37).

Who has ever sorrowed as Jesus did when He cried, *My soul is exceeding sorrowful, even unto death* (Matt. 26:38).

Who has an attitude of meekness that can compare with His? Who can so unashamedly say, *Come unto me, all ye that labour and are heavy laden, and I will give you rest. Take my yoke upon you, and learn of me; for I am meek and lowly in heart; and ye shall find rest unto your souls* (Matt. 11:28-29)? Of whom but Jesus could it be written, *Tell ye the daughter of Sion, Behold, thy King cometh unto thee, meek, and sitting upon an ass, and a colt the foal of an ass* (Matt. 21:5)?

No one has ever portrayed and demonstrated an attitude of hunger and thirst for righteousness more than Jesus. It was not that He needed righteousness for himself, however, for He is "the altogether righteous One," but it was for righteousness for all men, in particular for those who claim His name. Whose hunger and thirst for righteousness could ever match that of Him who was willing *to be made...sin for us...that we might be made the righteousness of God in him* (2 Cor. 5:21)? And of whom else could it be said so wholeheartedly, *Thou hast loved righteousness, and hated iniquity* (Heb. 1:9)?

Where else can such an attitude of mercy be found? Whose mercifulness can hold a candle to His? Of whom could it be so graciously stated, *...But according to his mercy he saved us, by the washing of regeneration, and renewing of* *the Holy Ghost; which he shed on us abundantly through Jesus Christ our Saviour* (Titus 3:5-6)?

And who else has ever so vicariously identified with the subjects of His mercy that it could be said of Him, *...in all things it behoved him to be made like unto his brethren, that he might be a merciful and faithful high priest in things pertaining to God, to make reconciliation for the sins of the people* (Heb. 2:17)?

And who would dare to equate his own purity of heart with that of our Lord? Whose attitude toward all evil even remotely approaches His? By the greatest stretch of any imagination, of whom else could it be so forthrightly declared, He is *holy, harmless, undefiled, separate from sinners, and made higher than the heavens* (Heb. 7:26)? Who could ever bear the description of His pristine Person set forth in the Revelation?

> *And I turned to see the voice that spake with me. And being turned, I saw seven golden candlesticks; and in the midst of the seven candlesticks one like unto the Son of man, clothed with a garment down to the foot, and girt about the paps with a golden girdle. His head and his hairs were white like wool, as white as snow; and his eyes were as a flame of fire; and his feet like unto fine brass, as if they burned in a furnace; and his voice as the sound of many waters. And he had in his right hand seven stars: and out of his mouth went a sharp twoedged sword: and his countenance was as the sun shineth in his strength.*
>
> (Rev. 1:12-16)

Who could more perfectly qualify for the designation of "peacemaker" than He? Who beside Him has ever been called the Prince of peace? And of whom else can it be said, *Of the increase of his government and peace there shall be no end* (Isa. 9:7)? Who has ever made such an effort for peace as He who *made peace through the blood of his cross* (Col. 1:20)? And who would venture to say, *Peace I leave with you, my peace I give unto you: not as the world giveth, give I unto you* (John 14:27)?

And, finally, who has been as persecuted for righteousness sake as He was? Who has been as reviled as He was, and has not reviled again? Who has been so *despised and rejected of men?* Who, like Him, has been of men esteemed *stricken, smitten of God, and afflicted* (Isa. 53:4)? Of whom, other than Jesus, has it ever been written that *...they bowed the knee before him, and mocked him, saying, Hail, King of the Jews!* (Matt. 27:29)? Upon whom have such false accusations been heaped?

There is but a single answer. There has never been another like Jesus. He is the embodiment of all of the attitudes of the Beatitudes. He is the ultimate of them all. He is the perfect blueprint for all who will be blessed.

Endnotes

1.. Quoted with permission by Dr. Norman Vincent Peale. *Reader's Digest* (1985).

2. Wuest, Kenneth. *The Gospels: An Expanded Translation.* (Grand Rapids, MI: Wm. B. Eerdmans Publishing Co.,1956).

3. Clarke, Adam. *Adam Clarke's Commentary.* (New York-Nashville: Abingdon-Cokesbury Press) Vol. 5, pp. 65.

4. *The Pulpit Commentary* (New York: Funk and Wagnalls Co.) Wartime Edition, Vol. 45, Second Corinthians, p. 188.

5. *The Pulpit Commentary* (New York: Funk and Wagnalls Co.) Wartime Edition, Vol. 33, St. Matthew, Vol. 1, p. 148.

6. Tozer, A. W. *The Pusuit of God*, (Harrisburg, PA: Christian Publications, Inc.) p. 113.

7. Bromiley, Geoffrey A. *Theological Dictionary of the New Testament* (Grand Rapids, MI: Wm B. Eerdmans Publishing Co, 1988) p. 172.

8. *The Pulpit Commentary* (New York: Funk and Wagnalls Co.) Wartime Edition, Vol. 33, St. Matthew, Vol. 1, p. 149.

9. Bromiley, Geoffrey A. *Theological Dictionary of the New Testament* (Grand Rapids, MI: Wm B. Eerdmans Publishing Co, 1988) p. 22.

10. *The International Standard Bible Dictionary.* (Grand Rapids, MI: Wm. B. Eerdmans Publishing Co.) p. 2033.

11. Clarke, Adam. *Adam Clarke's Commentary.* (New York-Nashville: Abingdon-Cokesbury Press) Vol. 5, pp. 65.

12. *The Pulpit Commentary* (New York: Funk and Wagnalls Co.) Wartime Edition, Vol. 46, Ephesians, p. 6.

13. *The Pulpit Commentary* (New York: Funk and Wagnalls Co.) Wartime Edition, Vol. 46, Galatians and Ephesians, p. 81.

14. *The Pulpit Commentary* (New York: Funk and Wagnalls Co.) Wartime Edition, Vol. 33, St. Matthew, Vol. 1, p. 179.

15. Henry, Matthew. *Matthew Henry's Commentary.* (New York: Fleming H. Revell Co., 1706) Vol. 5, Matthew to John.

16. *The Pulpit Commentary* (New York: Funk and Wagnalls Co.) Wartime Edition, Vol. 33, St. Matthew, Vol. 1, p. 175.